THE
GOOSE GIRL

HAROLD MACGRATH

1st WORLD
LIBRARY
Literary Society

The Goose Girl

Harold MacGrath

© 1st World Library, 2007
PO Box 2211
Fairfield, IA 52556
www.1stworldlibrary.com
First Edition

LCCN: 2007930791

Softcover ISBN: 978-1-4218-4834-1
Hardcover ISBN: 978-1-4218-4737-5
eBook ISBN: 978-1-4218-4931-7

Purchase *"The Goose Girl"*
as a traditional bound book at:
www.1stWorldLibrary.com/purchase.asp?ISBN=978-1-4218-4834-1

1st World Library is a literary, educational organization
dedicated to:

- Creating a free internet library of downloadable ebooks

- Hosting writing competitions and offering book publishing
scholarships.

Interested in more 1st World Library books? contact:
literacy@1stworldlibrary.com
Check us out at: www.1stworldlibrary.com

1ˢᵗ World Library Literary Society

Giving Back to the World

"If you want to work on the core problem, it's early school literacy."

- James Barksdale, former CEO of Netscape

"No skill is more crucial to the future of a child, or to a democratic and prosperous society, than literacy."

- Los Angeles Times

"Literacy... means far more than learning how to read and write... The aim is to transmit... knowledge and promote social participation."

- UNESCO

"Literacy is not a luxury, it is a right and a responsibility. If our world is to meet the challenges of the twenty-first century we must harness the energy and creativity of all our citizens."

- President Bill Clinton

"Parents should be encouraged to read to their children, and teachers should be equipped with all available techniques for teaching literacy, so the varying needs and capacities of individual kids can be taken into account."

- Hugh Mackay

CONTENTS

CHAPTER I

SOME IN RAGS

An old man, clothed in picturesque patches and tatters, paused and leaned on his stout oak staff. He was tired. He drew off his rusty felt hat, swept a sleeve across his forehead, and sighed. He had walked many miles that day, and even now the journey's end, near as it really was, seemed far away. Ah, but he would sleep soundly that night, whether the bed were of earth or of straw. His peasant garb rather enhanced his fine head. His eyes were blue and clear and far-seeing, the eyes of a hunter or a woodsman, of a man who watches the shadows in the forest at night or the dim, wavering lines on the horizon at daytime; things near or far or roundabout. His brow was high, his nose large and bridged; a face of more angles than contours, bristling with gray spikes, like one who has gone unshaven several days. His hands, folded over the round, polished knuckle of his staff, were tanned and soiled, but they were long and slender, and the callouses were pink, a certain indication that they were fresh.

The afternoon glow of the September sun burned along the dusty white highway. From where he stood the road trailed off miles behind and wound up five hundred feet or more above him to the ancient city of Dreiberg. It was not a steep road, but a long and weary one, a steady, enervating, unbroken climb. To the left the mighty cliff reared its granite side to the hanging city, broke in a wide plain, and then went on up several thousand feet to the ledges of dragon-green ice and snow. To the right sparkled and flashed a wild mountain stream on its way to the broad, fertile valley, which, mistily green and brown and yellow with vineyards and hops and corn, spread out and on to the north, stopping abruptly at the base of the more formidable chain of mountains.

Across this lofty jumble of barren rock and glacial cleft, now purpling and darkening as the sun mellowed in its decline, lay the kingdom of Jugendheit; and toward this the wayfarer gazed meditatively, absorbing little or nothing of the exquisite panorama. By and by his gaze wavered, and that particular patch in the valley, brown from the beating of many iron-shod horses, caught and chained his interest for a space. It was the military field, and it glittered and scintillated as squadron after squadron of cavalry dashed from side to side or wheeled in bewildering circles.

"The philosophy of war is to prepare for it," mused the old man, with a jerk of his shoulders. "France! So the mutter runs. There is a Napoleon in France, but no Bonaparte. Clatter-clatter! Bang-bang!" He laughed ironically and cautiously glanced at his watch, an article which must have cost him many and many a potato-patch. He pulled his hat over his eyes, scratched the irritating stubble on his chin, and stepped forward.

He had followed yonder goose-girl ever since the incline began. Oft the little wooden shoes had lagged, but here they were, still a hundred yards or more ahead of him. He had never been close enough to distinguish her features. The galloping of soldiers up and down the road from time to time disturbed her flock, but she was evidently a patient soul, and

Harold MacGrath

relied valiantly upon her stick of willow. Once or twice he had been inclined to hasten his steps, to join her, to talk, to hear the grateful sound of his own voice, which he had not heard since he passed the frontier customs; yet each time he had subdued the desire and continued to lessen none of the distance between them.

The little goose-girl was indeed tired, and the little wooden shoes grew heavier and heavier, and the little bare feet ached dully; but her heart was light and her mind sweet with happiness. Day after day she had tended the geese in the valley and trudged back at evening alone, all told a matter of twelve miles; and now she was bringing them into the city to sell in the market on the morrow. After that she would have little to do save an hour or two at night in a tavern called the Black Eagle, where she waited on patrons.

On the two went, the old man in tatters, the goose-girl in wooden shoes. The man listened; she was singing brightly, and the voice was sweet and strong and true.

"She is happy; that is some recompense. She is richer than I am." And the peasant fell into a reverie.

Presently there was a clatter of horses, a jingle of bit and spur and saber. The old man stepped to the side of the road and sat down on the stone parapet. It would be wiser now to wait till the dust settled. Half a dozen mounted officers trotted past. The peasant on the parapet instantly recognized one of the men. He saluted with a humbleness which lacked sincerity. It was the grand duke himself. There was General Ducwitz, too, and some of his staff, and a smooth-faced, handsome young man in civilian riding-clothes, who, though he rode like a cavalryman, was obviously of foreign birth, an Englishman or an American. They were laughing and chatting amiably, for the grand duke of Ehrenstein bothered himself about formalities only at formal times. The outsider watched them regretfully as they went by, and there was some envy in his heart, too.

When the cavalcade reached the goose-girl, the peace of the scene vanished forthwith. Confusion took up the scepter. The silly geese, instead of remaining on the left of the road, in safety, straightway determined that their haven of refuge was on the opposite side. Gonk-gonk! Quack-quack! They scrambled, they blundered, they flew. Some tried to go over the horses, some endeavored to go under. One landed, full-winged, against the grand duke's chest and swept his vizored cap off his head and rolled it into the dust. The duke signed to his companions to draw up; to proceed in this undignified manner was impossible. All laughed heartily, however; all excepting the goose-girl. To her it was far from being a laughing matter. It would take half an hour to calm her stupid charges. And she was *so* tired.

"Stupids!" she cried despairingly.

"From pigs and chickens, good Lord deliver us!" shouted the civilian, sliding from his horse and recovering the duke's cap.

Now, the duke was a kind-hearted, thoughtful man, notwithstanding his large and complex affairs of state; as he ceased laughing, he searched a pocket, and tossed a couple of coins to the forlorn goose-girl.

"I am sorry, little one," he said gravely. "I hope none of your geese is hurt."

"Oh, Highness!" cried the girl, breathless from her recent endeavors and overcome with the grandeur of the two ducal effigies in her hand. She had seen the grand duke times without number, but she had never yet been so near to him.

And now he had actually spoken to her. It was a miracle. She would tell them all that night in the dark old Krumerweg. And for the moment his prospect overshadowed all thought of her geese.

The civilian dusted the royal cap with his sleeve, returned it, and mounted. He then looked casually at the girl.

"By George!" he exclaimed, in English.

"What is it?" asked the duke, gathering up the reins.

"The girl's face; it is beautiful."

The duke, after a glance, readily agreed. "You Americans are always observant."

"Whenever there's a pretty face about," supplemented Ducwitz.

"I certainly shouldn't trouble to look at a homely one," the American retorted.

"Pretty figure, too," said one of the aides, a colonel. But his eye held none of the abstract admiration which characterized the American's.

The goose-girl had seen this look in other men's eyes; she knew. A faint color grew under her tan, and waned, but her eyes wavered not the breadth of a hair. It was the colonel who finally was forced to turn his gaze elsewhere, chagrined. His face was not unfamiliar to her.

"Beauty is a fickle goddess," remarked Ducwitz tritely, settling himself firmly in the saddle. "In giving, she is as blind as a bat. I know a duchess now - but never mind."

"Let us be going forward," interrupted the duke. There were more vital matters under hand than the beauty of a strolling goose-girl.

So the troop proceeded with dust and small thunder, and shortly passed the city gates, which in modern times were never closed. It traversed the lumpy cobbles of the narrow streets, under hanging gables, past dim little shops and markets, often unintentionally crowding pedestrians into doorways or against the walls. One among those so inconvenienced was a youth dressed as a vintner. He was tall, pliantly built, blond as a Viking, possessing a singular beauty of the masculine order. He was forced to flatten himself against the wall of a house, his arms extended on either side, in a kind of temporary crucifixion. Even then the stirrup of the American touched him slightly. But it was not the touch of the stirrup that startled him; it was the dark, clean-cut face of the rider. Once they were by, the youth darted into a doorway.

"He? What can he be doing here? No, it is utterly impossible; it is merely a likeness."

He ventured forth presently, none of the perturbation, however, gone from his face. He ran his hand across his chin; yes, he would let his beard grow.

The duke and his escort turned into the broad and restful sweep of the Koenig Strasse, with its fashionable residences, shops, cafes and hotels. At the end of the *Strasse* was the Ehrenstein Platz, the great square round which ran the palaces and the royal and public gardens. On the way many times the duke raised his hand in salutations; for, while not exactly loved, he was liked for his rare clean living, his sound sense of justice and his honest efforts to do what was right. Opera-singers came and went, but none had ever penetrated into the private suites of the palace. The halt was made in the courtyard, and all dismounted.

The American thanked the duke gratefully for the use of the horse.

"You are welcome to a mount at all times, Mr. Carmichael," replied the duke pleasantly. "A man who rides as well as yourself may be trusted anywhere with any kind of a horse."

The group looked admiringly at the object of this marked attention. Here was one who had seen two years of constant and terrible warfare, who had ridden horses under fire, and who bore on his body many honorable scars. For the great civil strife in America had come to its close but two years before, and Europe was still captive to her amazement at the military prowess of the erstwhile inconsiderable American.

As Carmichael saluted and turned to leave the courtyard, he threw a swift, searching glance at one of the palace windows. Did the curtain stir? He could not say. He continued on, crossing the Platz, toward the Grand Hotel. He was a bachelor, so he might easily have had his quarters at the consulate; but as usual with American consulates - even to the present time - it was situated in an undesirable part of the town, over a *Bierhalle* frequented by farmers and the middle class. Having a moderately comfortable income of his own, he naturally preferred living at the Grand Hotel.

Where had he seen that young vintner before?

* * * * *

Meanwhile, the goose-girl set resolutely about the task of remarshaling her awkward squad. With a soft, clucking sound she moved hither and thither. A feather or two drifted lazily about in the air. At last she gathered them in, all but one foolish, blank-eyed gander, which, poising on a large boulder, threatened to dive headforemost into the torrent. She coaxed him gently, then severely, but without success. The old man in patches came up.

"Let me get him for you, *Kindchen*," he volunteered.

The good-fellowship in his voice impressed her far more than the humble state of his dress. But she smiled and shook her head.

"It is dangerous," she affirmed. "It will be wiser to wait. In a little while he will come down of his own accord."

"Bah!" cried the old man. "It is nothing; I am a mountaineer."

In spite of his weariness, he proved himself to be a dexterous climber. Foot by foot he crawled up the side of the huge stone. A slip, and his life would not have been worth one of the floating feathers. The gander saw him coming and stirred uneasily. Nearer and nearer came this human spider. The gander flapped its wings, but hesitated to take the leap. Instantly a brown hand shot up and caught the scaly yellow legs. There was much squawking on the way down, but when his gandership saw his more tractable brothers and sisters peacefully waddling up the road, he subsided and took his place in the ranks without more ado.

"You are a brave man, Herr." There was admiration in the girl's eyes.

"To court danger and to overcome obstacles is a part of my regular business. I do not know what giddiness is. You are welcome to the service. It is a long walk from the valley."

Harold MacGrath

"I have walked it many times this summer. But this is the last day. To-morrow I sell the geese in the market to the hotels. They have all fine livers" - lightly touching a goose with her willow stick.

"What, the hotels?" - humorously.

"No, no, my geese!"

"What was that song you were singing before the horses came up?"

"That? It was from the poet Heine" - simply.

He stared at her with a rudeness not at all intentional.

"Heine? Can you read?"

"Yes, Herr."

The other walked along beside her in silence. After all, why not? Why should he be surprised? From one end of the world to the other printer's ink was spreading and bringing light. But a goose-girl who read Heine!

"And the music?" he inquired presently.

"That is mine" - with the first sign of diffidence. "Melodies are always running through my head. Sometimes they make me forget things I ought to remember."

"Your own music? An impresario will be discovering you some fine day, and your fortune will be made."

The light irony did not escape her. "I am only a goose-girl."

He felt disarmed. "What is your name?"

"Gretchen."

"What else?"

"Nothing else" - wistfully. "I never knew any father or mother."

"So?" This was easier for the other to understand. "But who taught you to read?"

"A priest. Once I lived in the mountains, at an inn. He used to come in evenings, when the snow was not too deep. He taught me to read and write, and many things besides. I know that Italy has all the works of art; that France has the most interesting history; that Germany has all the philosophers, and America all the money," adding a smile. "I should like to see America. Sometimes I find a newspaper, and I read it all through."

"History?"

"A little, and geography."

"With all this wide learning you ought to be something better than a tender of geese."

"It is honest work, and that is good."

"I meant nothing wrong, *Kindchen*. But you would find it easier in a milliner's shop, as a lady's maid, something of that order."

"With these?" - holding out her hands.

Harold MacGrath

"It would not take long to whiten them. Do you live alone?"

"No. I live with my foster-mother, who is very old. I call her grandmother. She took me in when I was a foundling; now I am taking care of her. She has always been good to me. And what might your name be?"

"Ludwig."

"Ludwig what?" - inquisitive in her turn.

"Oh, the other does not matter. I am a mountaineer from Jugendheit."

"Jugendheit?" She paused to look at him more closely. "We are not friendly with your country."

"More's the pity. It is a grave blunder on the part of the grand duke. There is a mote in his eye."

"Wasn't it all about the grand duke's daughter?"

"Yes. But she has been found. Yet the duke is as bitter as of old. He is wrong, he was always wrong." The old man spoke with feeling. "What is this new-found princess like?"

"She is beautiful and kind."

"So?"

The geese were behaving, and only occasionally was she obliged to use her stick. And as her companion asked no more questions, she devoted her attention to the flock, proud of their broad backs and full breasts.

On his part, he observed her critically, for he was more than curious now, he was interested. She was not tall, but her lithe slenderness gave her the appearance of tallness. Her hands, rough-nailed and sunburnt, were small and shapely; the bare foot in the wooden shoe might have worn without trouble Cinderella's magic slipper. Her clothes, coarse and homespun, were clean and variously mended. Her hair, in a thick braid, was the tone of the heart of a chestnut-bur, and her eyes were of that mystifying hazel, sometimes brown, sometimes gray, according to whether the sky was clear or overcast. And there was something above and beyond all these things, a modesty, a gentleness and a purity; none of the bold, rollicking, knowing manner so common in handsome peasant girls. He contemplated her through half-closed eyes and gave her in fancy the tariffing furbelows of a woman of fashion; she would have been beautiful.

"How old are you, Gretchen?"

"I do not know," she answered, "perhaps eighteen, perhaps twenty."

Again they went forward in silence. By the time they reached the gates the sun was no longer visible on the horizon, but it had gone down ruddy and uncrowned by any cloud, giving promise of a fair day on the morrow. The afterglow on the mountains across the valley was now in its prime glory; and once the two wayfarers paused and commented upon it. Once more the mountaineer was agreeably surprised; the average peasant is impervious to atmospheric splendor, beauty carries no message.

Arriving at length in the city, they passed through the crooked streets, sometimes so narrow that the geese were packed from wall to wall. Oft some jovial soldier sent a jest or a query to them across the now gray backs of the geese. But Gretchen looked on ahead, purely and serenely.

"Gretchen, where shall I find the Adlergasse?"

"We pass through it shortly. I will show you. You are also a stranger in Dreiberg?"

"Yes."

They took the next turn, and the weather-beaten sign *Zum Schwartzen Adler*, hanging in front of a frame house of many gables, caused the mountaineer to breathe gratefully.

"Here my journey ends, Gretchen. The Black Eagle," he added, in an undertone; "it is unchanged these twenty years. Heaven send that the beds are softer than aforetime!"

They were passing a clock-mender's shop. The man from Jugendheit peered in the window, which had not been cleaned in an age, but there was no clock in sight to give him warning of the time, and he dared not now look at his watch. He had a glimpse of the ancient clock-mender himself, however, huddled over a table upon which sputtered a candle. It touched up his face with grotesque lights. Here was age, mused the man outside the window; nothing less than fourscore years rested upon those rounded shoulders. The face was corrugated with wrinkles, like a frosted road; eyes heavily spectacled, a ragged thatch of hair on the head, a ragged beard on the chin. Aware of a shadow between him and the fading daylight, the clock-mender looked up from his work. The eyes of the two men met, but only for a moment.

The mountaineer, who felt rejuvenated by this contrast, straightened his shoulders and started to cross the street to the tavern.

"Good night, Gretchen. Good luck to you and your geese to-morrow."

"Thanks, Herr Ludwig. And will you be long in the city?"

"That depends; perhaps," adding a grim smile in answer to a grim thought.

He offered his hand, which she accepted trustfully. He was a strange old man, but she liked him. When she withdrew her hand, something cold and hard remained in her palm. Wonders of all the world! It was a piece of gold. Her eyes went up quickly, but the giver smiled reassuringly and put a finger against his lips.

"But, Herr," she remonstrated.

"Keep it; I give it to you. Do not question providence, and I am her handmaiden just now. Go along with you."

So Gretchen in a mild state of stupefaction turned away. Clat-clat! sang the little wooden shoes. A plaintive gonk rose as she prodded a laggard from the dank gutter. A piece of gold! Clat-clat! Clat-clat! Surely this had been a day of marvels; two crowns from the grand duke and a piece of gold from this old man in peasant clothes. Instinctively she knew that he was not a peasant. But what could he be? Comparison would have made him a king. She was too tired and hungry to make further deductions.

She was regarded with kindly eyes till the dark jaws of the Krumerweg swallowed up both her and her geese.

"Poor little goose-girl!" he thought. "If she but knew, she could make a bonfire of a thousand hearts. A fine day!" He eyed again the battered sign. It was then that he discerned another, leaning from the ledge of the first story of the house adjoining the tavern. It was the tarnished shield of the United States.

Harold MacGrath

"What a penurious government it must be! Two weeks, tramping about the country in this unholy garb, following false trails half the time, living on crusts and cold meats. Ah, you have led me a merry dance, nephew, but I shall not forget!"

He entered the tavern and applied for a room, haggling over the price.

CHAPTER II

AN AMERICAN CONSUL

The nights in Dreiberg during September are often chill. The heavy mists from the mountain slip down the granite clifts and spread over the city, melting all sharp outlines, enfeebling the gas-lamps, and changing the moon, if there happens to be one, into something less than a moon and something more than a pewter disk. And so it was this night.

Carmichael, in order to finish his cigar on the little balcony fronting his window, found it necessary to put on his light overcoat, though he perfectly knew that he was in no manner forced to smoke on the balcony. But the truth was he wanted a clear vision of the palace and the lighted windows thereof, and of one in particular. He had no more sense than Tom-fool, the abetter of follies. She was as far removed from him as the most alien of the planets; but the magnet shall ever draw the needle, and a woman shall ever draw a man. He knew that it was impossible, that it grew more impossible day by day, and he railed at himself bitterly and satirically.

He sighed and teetered his legs. A sigh moves nothing forward, yet it is as essential as life itself. It is the safety-valve to every emotion; it is the last thing in laughter, the last thing in tears. One sighs in entering the world and in leaving it, perhaps in protest. A child sighs for the moon because it knows no better. Carmichael sighed for the Princess Hildegarde, understanding. It was sigh or curse, and the latter mode of expression wastes more vitality. Oh, yes; they made over him, as the world goes; they dined and wined him and elected him honorary member to their clubs; they patted him on the back and called him captain; but it was all in a negligent toleration that turned every pleasure into rust.

Arthur Carmichael was Irish. He was born in America, educated there and elsewhere, a little while in Paris, a little while at Bonn, and, like all Irishmen, he was baned with the wandering foot; for the man who is homeless by choice has a subtle poison in his blood. He was at Bonn when the Civil War came. He went back to America and threw himself into the fight with all the ardor that had made his forebears famous in the service of the worthless Stuarts. It wasn't a question with him of the mere love of fighting, of tossing the penny; he knew with which side he wished to fight. He joined the cavalry of the North, and hammered and fought his way to a captaincy. He was wounded five times and imprisoned twice. His right eye was still weak from the effects of a powder explosion; and whenever it bothered him he wore a single glass, abominating, as all soldiers do, the burden of spectacles. At the end of the conflict he returned to Washington.

And then the inherent curse put a hand on his shoulder; he must be moving. His parents were dead; there was no anchor, nor had lying ambition enmeshed him. There was a little property, the income from which was enough for his wants. Without any influence whatever, save his pleasing address and his wide education, he blarneyed the State Department out of a consulate. They sent him to Ehrenstein, at a salary not worth mentioning, with the diplomatic halo of dignity as a tail to the kite. He had been in the service some two years by now, and those who knew him well rather wondered at his sedative turn of mind. Two years in any one place was not in reckoning as regarded Carmichael; yet, here he was, caring neither for promotion nor exchange. So, then, all logical deductions simmered down to one: *Cherchez la femme*.

He knew that his case would never be tried in court nor settled out of it; and he realized that it would be far better to weigh anchor and set his course for other parts. But no man ever quite forsakes his dream-woman; and he had endued a princess with all the shining attributes of an angel, when, had he known it, she was only angelic.

The dreamer is invariably tripping over his illusions; and Carmichael was rather boyish in his dreams. What absurd romances he was always weaving round her! What exploits on her behalf! But never anything happened, and never was the grand duke called upon to offer his benediction.

It was all very foolish and romantic and impossible, and no one recognized this more readily than he. No American ever married a princess of a reigning house, and no American ever will. This law is as immovable as the law of gravitation. Still, man is master of his dreams, and he may do as he pleases in the confines of this small circle. Outside these temporary lapses, Carmichael was a keen, shrewd, far-sighted young man, close-lipped and observant, never forgetting faces, never forgetting benefits, loving a fight but never provoking one. So he and the world were friends. Diplomacy has its synonym in tact, and he was an able tactician, for all that an Irishman is generally likened to a bull in a china-shop.

"How the deuce will it end?" - musing half aloud. "I'll forget myself some day and trip so hard that they'll be asking

Harold MacGrath

Washington for my recall. I'll go over to the gardens and listen to the band. They are playing dirges to-night, and anything funereal will be a light and happy tonic to my present state of mind."

He was standing on the curb in front of the hotel, his decision still unrounded, when he noticed a closed carriage hard by the fountain in the Platz. The driver dozed on his box.

"Humph! There's a man who is never troubled with counting the fool's beads. Silver and copper are his gods and goddesses. Ha! a fare!"

A woman in black, thoroughly veiled and cloaked, came round from the opposite side of the fountain. She spoke to the driver, and he tumbled off the box, alive and hearty. There seemed to be a short interchange of words of mutual satisfaction. The lady stepped into the carriage, the driver woke up his ancient Bucephalus, and went clickety-clack down the Koenig Strasse toward the town.

To Carmichael it was less than an incident. He twirled his cane and walked toward the public gardens. Here he strolled about, watching the people, numerous but orderly, with a bright military patch here and there. The band struck up again, and he drifted with the crowd toward the pavilion. The penny-chairs were occupied, so he selected a spot off-side, near enough for all auditual purposes. One after another he carelessly scanned the faces of those nearest. He was something of an amateur physiognomist, but he seldom made the mistakes of the tyro.

Within a dozen feet of him, her arms folded across her breast, her eyes half shut in the luxury of the senses, stood the goose-girl. He smiled as he recalled the encounter of that afternoon. It was his habit to ride to the maneuvers every day, and several times he had noticed her, as well as any rider is able to notice a pedestrian. But that afternoon her beauty came home to him suddenly and unexpectedly. Had she been other than what she was, a woman well-gowned, for instance, riding in her carriage, his interest would have waned in the passing. But it had come with the same definite surprise as when one finds a rare and charming story in a dilapidated book.

"Why couldn't I have fallen in love with some one like this?" he cogitated.

With a friendly smile on his lips, he took a step toward her, but instantly paused. Colonel von Wallenstein of the general staff approached her from the other side, and Carmichael was curious to find out what that officer's object was. Wallenstein was a capital soldier, and a jolly fellow round a board, but beyond that Carmichael had no real liking for him. There were too many scented notes stuck in his pockets.

The colonel dropped his cigarette, leaned over Gretchen's shoulder and spoke a few words. At first she gave no heed. The colonel persisted. Without a word in reply, she resolutely sought the nearest policeman. Wallenstein, remaining where he was, laughed. Meantime the policeman frowned. It was incredible; his excellency could not possibly have intended any wrong, it was only a harmless pleasantry. Gretchen's lips quivered; the law of redress in Ehrenstein had no niche for the goose-girl.

"Good evening, colonel," said Carmichael pleasantly. "Why can't your bandmaster give us light opera once in a while?"

The colonel pulled his mustache in chagrin, but he did not give Carmichael the credit for bringing about this cheapening sense. For the time being Gretchen was freed from annoyance.

Harold MacGrath

The colonel certainly could not rush off to her and give this keen-eyed American an opportunity to witness a further rebuff.

"Light operas are rare at present," he replied, accepting his defeat amiably enough.

"Paris is full of them just now," continued Carmichael.

"Paris? Would you like a riot in the gardens?" asked the colonel, amused.

"A riot?" said Carmichael derisively. "Why, nothing short of a bombshell would cause a riot among your phlegmatic Germans."

"I believe you love your Paris better than your Dreiberg."

"Not a bit of doubt. And down in your heart you do, too. Think of the lights, the theaters, the cafes and the pretty women!" Carmichael's cane described a flourish as if to draw a picture of these things.

"Yes, yes," agreed the colonel reminiscently; "you are right. There is no other night equal to a Parisian night. *Ach, Gott!* But think of the mornings, think of the mornings!" - dolefully.

"On the contrary, let us not think of them!" - with a mock shudder.

And then a pretty woman rose from a chair near-by. She nodded brightly at the colonel, who bowed, excused himself to Carmichael, and made off after her.

"I believe I stepped on his toe that time," said Carmichael to himself.

Then he looked round for Gretchen. She was still at the side of the policeman. She had watched the scene between the two men, but was quite unconscious that it had been set for her benefit. She came back. Carmichael stepped confidently to her side and raised his hat.

"Did you get your geese together without mishap?" he asked.

The instinct of the child always remains with the woman. Gretchen smiled. This young man would be different, she knew.

"They were only frightened. But his highness" - eagerly - "was he very angry?"

"Angry? Not the least. He was amused. But he was nearly knocked off his horse. If you lived in America now, you might reap a goodly profit from that goose."

"America? How?"

"You could put him in a museum and exhibit him as an intimate friend of the grand duke of Ehrenstein."

But Gretchen did not laugh. It was a serious thing to talk lightly of so grand a person as the duke. Still, the magic word America, where the gold came from, flamed her curiosity.

"You are from America?"

"Yes."

"Are you rich?"

"In fancy, in dreams" - humorously.

"Oh! I thought they were all rich."

"Only one or two of us."

"Is it very large, this America?"

"France, Spain, Prussia would be lonesome if set down in America. Only Russia has anything to boast of."

"Did you fight in the war?"

"Yes. Do you like music?"

"Were you ever wounded?"

"A scratch or two, nothing to speak of. But do you like music?"

"Very, very much. When they play Beethoven, Bach, or Meyerbeer, *ach*, I seem to live in another country. I hear music in everything, in the leaves, the rain, the wind, the stream."

It seemed strange to him that he had not noticed it at first, the almost Hanoverian purity of her speech and the freedom with which she spoke. The average peasant is diffident, with a vocabulary of few words, ignorant of art or music or where the world lay.

"What is your name?"

"Gretchen."

"It is a good name; it is famous, too."

"Goethe used it."

"So he did." Carmichael ably concealed his surprise: "You have some one who reads to you?"

"No, Herr. I can read and write and do sums in addition."

He was willing to swear that she was making fun of him. Was she a simple goose-girl? Was she not something more, something deeper? War-clouds were forming in the skies; they might gather and strike at any time. And who but the French could produce such a woman spy? Ehrenstein was not Prussia, it was true; but the duchy with its twenty thousand troops was one of the many pulses that beat in unison with this man Bismarck's plans. Carmichael addressed her quickly in French, aiming to catch her off her guard.

"I do not speak French, Herr," - honestly.

He was certainly puzzled, but a glance at her hands dissolved his doubts. These hands were used to toil, they were in no way disguised. No Frenchwoman would sacrifice her hands for her country; at least, not to this extent. Yet the two things in his mind would not readily cohese: a goose-girl who was familiar with the poets and composers.

"You have been to school?"

"After a manner. My teacher was a kind priest. But he never knew that, with knowledge, he was to open the gates of discontent."

"Then you are not happy with your lot?"

"Is any one, Herr?" - quietly. "And who might you be, and what might you be doing here in Dreiberg, riding with the grand duke?"

"I am the American consul."

Gretchen took a step back.

"Oh, it is nothing that will bite you," he added.

"But perhaps I have been disrespectful!"

"Pray, how?"

Gretchen found that she had no definite explanation to offer.

"What did Colonel Wallenstein say to you?"

"Nothing of importance. I am used to it. I am perfectly able to take care of myself," she answered.

"But he annoyed you."

"That is true," she admitted.

"What did the policeman say?"

"What would he say to a goose-girl?"

"Shall I speak to him?"

"Would it really do any good?" - skeptically.

"It might. The duke is friendly toward me, and I am certain he would not tolerate such conduct in his police."

"You would only make enemies for me; insolence would become persecution. I know. Yet, I thank you, Herr - "

"Carmichael. Now, listen, Gretchen; if at any time you are in trouble, you will find me at the Grand Hotel or at the consulate next door to the Black Eagle."

"I shall remember. Sometimes I work in the Black Eagle." And recollection rose in her mind of the old man who had given her the gold piece.

"Good night," he said.

"Thank you, Herr."

Gretchen extended her hand and Carmichael took it in his own, inspecting it.

"Why do you do that?"

"It is a good hand; it is strong, too."

"It has to be strong, Herr. Good night."

Carmichael raised his hat again, and Gretchen breathed contentedly as she saw him disappear in the crowd. That little act of courtesy made everything brighter. There was only one other who ever touched his hat to her respectfully. And as she stood there, dreaming over the unusual happenings of the day, she felt an arm slip through hers, gently but firmly, even with authority. Her head went round.

"Leo?" she whispered.

The young vintner whom Carmichael had pushed against the wall that day smiled from under the deep shade of his hat, drawn down well over his face.

"Gretchen, who was that speaking to you?"

"Herr Carmichael, the American consul."

"Carmichael!" The arm in Gretchen's stiffened.

"What is it, Leo?"

"Nothing. Only, I grow mad with rage when any of these gentlemen speak to you. Gentlemen! I know them all too well."

"This one means no harm."

"I would I were certain. Ah, how I love you!" he whispered.

Gretchen thrilled and drew his arm closely against her side.

"To me the world began but two weeks ago. I have just begun to live."

"I am glad," said Gretchen. "But listen."

The band was playing again.

"Sometimes I am jealous even of that."

"I love you none the less for loving it."

"I know; but I am sad and lonely to-night" - gloomily. "I want all your thoughts."

"Are they not always yours? And why should you be sad and miserable?"

"Why, indeed!"

"Leo, as much as I love you, there is always a shadow."

"What shadow?"

"It is always at night that I see you, rarely in the bright daytime. What do you do during the day? It is not yet vintage. What do you do?"

"Will you trust me a little longer, Gretchen, just a little longer?"

"Always, not a little longer, always. But wait till the music stops and I will tell you of my adventure."

"You have had an adventure?" - distrustfully.

"Yes. Be still."

There were tones in Gretchen's voice that the young vintner could never quite understand. There was a will little less than imperial, and often as he rebelled, he never failed to bow to it.

"What was this adventure?" he demanded, as the music stopped.

She told him about the geese, the grand duke, and the two crowns. He laughed, and she joined him, for it was amusing now.

The musicians were putting away their instruments, the crowd was melting, the attendants were stacking the chairs, so the two lovers went out of the gardens toward the town and the Krumerweg.

Meanwhile Carmichael had lectured the policeman, who was greatly disturbed.

"Your Excellency, I am sure Colonel von Wallenstein meant

no harm."

"Are you truthfully sure?"

The policeman plucked at his beard nervously. "It is every man for himself, as your excellency knows. Had I spoken to the colonel, he would have had me broken."

"You could have appealed to the duke."

"Perhaps. I am sorry for the girl, but I have a family to take care of."

"Well, mark me; this little woman loves music; she comes here often. The next time she is annoyed by Wallenstein or any one else, you report it to me. I'll see that it reaches his highness."

"I shall gladly do that, your Excellency."

Carmichael left the gardens and wandered with aimless step. He was surprised to find that he was opposite the side gates to the royal gardens. His feet had followed the bent of his mind. Yet he did not cross the narrow side street. The sound of carriage wheels caused him to halt. He waited. The carriage he had seen by the fountain drew up before the gates, and the woman in black alighted. She spoke to the sentinel, who opened the gates and closed them. The veiled lady vanished abruptly beyond the shrubbery.

"I wonder who that was?" was Carmichael's internal question. "Bah! Some lady-in-waiting with an affair on hand."

CHAPTER III

FOR HER COUNTRY

"Count, must I tell you again not to broach that subject? There can be no alliance between Ehrenstein and Jugendheit."

"Why?" asked Count von Herbeck, chancellor, coolly returning the angry flash from the ducal eyes.

"There are a thousand reasons why, but it is not my purpose to name them."

"Name only one, your Highness, only one."

"Will that satisfy you?"

"Perhaps."

"One of my reasons is that I do not want any alliance with a country so perfidious as Jugendheit. What! I make overtures? I, who have been so cruelly wronged all these years? You are mad."

"But what positive evidence have you that Jugendheit wronged you?"

Harold MacGrath

"Positive? Have I eyes and ears? Have I not seen and read and heard?" This time the duke struck the desk savagely. "Why do you always rouse me in this fashion, Herbeck? You know how distasteful all this is to me."

"Your highness knows that I look only to the welfare of the country. In the old days it was a foregone conclusion that this alliance was to be formed. Now, you persist in averring that the late king was the chief conspirator in abducting her serene highness, aided by Arnsberg, whose successor I have the honor to be. I have never yet seen any proofs. You have never yet produced them. Show me something which absolutely convicts them, and I'll surrender."

"On your honor?"

"My word."

The grand duke struck the bell on the chancellor's desk.

"My secretary, and tell him to bring me the packet marked A. He will understand."

The two men waited without speaking, each busy with thought. The duke had been in his youth, and was still, a handsome man, splendidly set up, healthy and vigorous, keen mentally, and whatever stubbornness he possessed nicely balanced by common sense. He might have been guilty in his youth of a few human peccadillos, but the kingly and princely excesses which at that time were making the east side of the Rhine the scandal of the world had in no wise sullied his name. Ehrenstein means "stone of honor," and he had always carried the thought of this in his heart. He was frank in his likes and dislikes, he hated secrets, and he loved an opponent who engaged him in the open. Herbeck often labored with him over this open manner, but the mind he sought to work upon was as receptive to political hypocrisy as a wall of granite. It was this extraordinary rectitude which made the duke so powerful an aid to Bismarck in the days that followed. The Man of Iron needed this sort of character as a cover and a buckler to his own duplicities.

Herbeck was an excellent foil. He was as silent and secretive as sand. He moved, as it were, in circles, thus always eluding dangerous corners. He was tall, angular, with a thin, immobile countenance, well guarded by his gray eyes and straight lips. He was a born financier, with almost limitless ambition, though only he himself knew how far this ambition reached. He had not brought prosperity to Ehrenstein, but he had fortified and bastioned it against extravagance, and this was probably the larger feat of the two. He loved his country, and brooded over it as a mother broods over her child. Twice had he saved Ehrenstein from the drag-net of war, and with honor. So he was admired by fathers and revered by mothers.

The secretary came in and laid a thin packet of papers on the chancellor's desk. "It was the packet A, your Highness?" - his hand still resting upon the documents.

"Yes. You may go."

The secretary bowed and withdrew.

The duke stirred the papers angrily, took one of them and spread it out with a rasp.

"Look at that. Whose writing, I ask?"

Herbeck adjusted his glasses and scrutinized the slanting hieroglyphics. He ran over it several times. At length he opened a drawer in his desk, sorted some papers, and brought out a yellow letter. This he laid down beside the other.

"Yes, they are alike. This will be Arnsberg. But" - mildly - "who may say that it is not a cunning forgery?"

"Forgery!" roared the duke. "Read this one from the late king of Jugendheit to Arnsberg, then, if you still doubt."

Herbeck read slowly and carefully.

Then he rose and walked to the nearest window, studying the letter again in the sharper light. Presently his hands fell behind his back and met about the paper, while he himself stared over into the royal gardens. He remained in this attitude for some time.

"Well?" said the duke impatiently.

Herbeck returned to his chair. "I wish that you had shown me these long ago."

"To what end?"

"You accused the king?"

"Certainly, but he denied it."

"In a letter?"

"Yes. Here, read it."

Herbeck compared the two. "Where did you find these?"

"In Arnsberg's desk," returned the duke, the anger in his eyes giving place to gloomy retrospection. "Arnsberg, my boyhood playmate, the man I loved and trusted and advanced to the highest office in my power. Is that not the way? Do we ever trust any one fully without being in the end deceived?

Well, dead or alive," the duke continued, his throat swelling, "ten thousand crowns to him who brings Arnsberg to me, dead or alive."

"He will never come back," said Herbeck.

"Not if he is wise. He was clever. He sent all his fortune to Paris, so I found, and what I confiscated was nothing but his estate. But do you believe me" - putting a hand against his heart - "something here tells me that some day fate will drag him back and give him into my hands?"

"You are very bitter."

"And have I not cause? Did not my wife die of a broken heart, and did I not become a broken man? You do not know all, Herbeck, not quite all. Franz also sought the hand of the Princess Sofia. He, too, loved her, but I won. Well, his revenge must have been sweet to him."

"But your daughter has been restored to her own."

"Due to your indefatigable efforts alone. Ah, Herbeck, nothing will ever fill up the gap between, nothing will ever restore the mother." The duke bowed his head.

Herbeck studied him thoughtfully.

"I love my daughter and she loves me, but I don't know what it is, I can't explain it," irresolutely.

"What can not your highness explain?"

"Perhaps the gap is too wide, perhaps the separation has been too long."

Herbeck did not press the duke to be more explicit. He opened another drawer and took forth a long hood envelope, crested and sealed.

"Your Highness, here is a letter from the prince regent of Jugendheit, formally asking the hand of the Princess Hildegarde for his nephew, Frederick, who will shortly be crowned. My advice is to accept, to let bygones be bygones."

"Write the prince that I respectfully decline."

"Do nothing in haste, your Highness. Temporize; say that you desire some time to think about the matter. You can change your mind at any time. A reply like this commits you to nothing, whereas your abrupt refusal will only widen the breach."

"The wider the breach the better."

"No, no, your Highness; the past has disturbed you. We can stand war, and it is possible that we might win, even against Jugendheit; but war at this late day would be a colossal blunder. Victory would leave us where we began thirty years ago. One does not go to war for a cause that has been practically dead these sixteen years. And an insult to Jugendheit might precipitate war. It would be far wiser to let me answer the prince regent, saying that your highness will give the proposal your thoughtful consideration."

"Have your way, then, but on your head be it if you commit me to anything."

The duke was about to gather up his documentary evidence, when Herbeck touched his hand.

"I have an idea," said the chancellor. "A great many letters reach me from day to day. I have an excellent memory. Who knows but that I might find the true conspirator, the archplotter? Leave them with me, your Highness."

"I shall not ask you to be careful with them, Herbeck."

"I shall treasure them as my life."

The duke departed, stirred as he had not been since the restoration of the princess. Herbeck sometimes irritated him, for he was never in the wrong, he was never impatient, he was never hasty, he never had to go over a thing twice. This supernal insight, which overlooked all things but results, set the duke wondering if Herbeck was truly all human. If only he could catch him at fault once in a while!

Count von Herbeck remained at his desk, his face as inscrutable as ever, his eyes without expression, and his lips expressing nothing. He smoothed out a sheet of paper, affixed the state seal, and in a flowing hand wrote a diplomatic note, considering the proposal of his royal highness, the prince regent of Jugendheit, on behalf of his nephew, the king. This he placed in the diplomatic pouch, called for a courier, and despatched him at once for the frontier.

The duke sought his daughter. She was in the music-room, surrounded by several of her young women companions, each holding some musical instrument in her hands. Hildegarde was singing. The duke paused, shutting his eyes and striving to recall the voice of the mother. When the voice died away and the young women leaned back in their chairs to rest, the duke approached. Upon seeing him all rose. With a smile he dismissed them.

"My child," he began, taking Hildegarde's hand and drawing

her toward a window-seat, "the king of Jugendheit asks for your hand."

"Mine, father?"

"Even so."

"Then I am to marry the king of Jugendheit?" There was little joy in her voice.

"Ah, we have not gone so far as that. The king, through his uncle, has simply made a proposal. How would you regard it, knowing what you do of the past, the years that you lived in comparative penury, amid hardships, unknown, and almost without name?"

"It is for you to decide, father. Whatever your decision is, I shall abide by it."

"It is a hard lesson we have to learn, my child. We can not always marry where we love; diplomacy and politics make other plans. But fortunately for you you love no one yet." He put his hand under her chin and searched the deeps of her gray eyes. These eyes were more like her mother's than anything else about her. "The king is young, handsome, they say, and rich. Politically speaking, it would be a great match."

"I am in your hands. You know what is best."

The duke was poignantly disappointed. Why did she not refuse outright, indignantly, contemptuously, as became one of the House of Ehrenstein? Anything rather than this complacency.

"What is he like?" disengaging his hand and turning her face toward the window.

"That no one seems to know. He has been to his capital but twice in ten years, which doubtless pleased his uncle, who loves power for its own sake. The young king has been in Paris most of the time. That's the way they educate kings these days. They teach them all the vices and make virtue an accident. Your father loves you, and if you are inclined toward his majesty, if it is in your heart to become a queen, I shall not let my prejudices stand in the way."

She caught up his hand with a strange passion and kissed it.

"Father, I do not want to marry any one," wistfully. "But a queen!" she added thoughtfully.

"It is only a sound, my dear; do not let it delude you. Herbeck advises this alliance, and while I realize that his judgment is right, my whole soul revolts against it. But all depends upon you."

"Would it benefit the people? Would it be for the good of the state?"

Here was reason. "Yes; my objections are merely personal," said the duke.

"For the good of my country, which I love, I am ready to make any sacrifice. I shall think it over."

"Very well; but weigh the matter carefully. There is never any retracing a step of this kind." He stood up, his heart heavy. Saying no more, he moved toward the door.

She gazed after him, and suddenly and silently she stretched out her arms, her eyes and face and lips yearning with love.

Harold MacGrath

Curiously enough, the duke happened to turn. He was at her side in a moment, holding her firm in his embrace.

"You are all I have, girl!" with a bit of break in his voice.

"My father!" She stroked his cheek.

When he left the room it was with lighter step.

The restoration of the Princess Hildegarde of Ehrenstein had been the sensation of Europe, as had been in the earlier days her remarkable abduction. For sixteen years the search had gone on fruitlessly. The cleverest adventuresses on the continent tried devious tricks to palm themselves off as the lost princess. From France they had come, from Prussia, Italy, Austria, Russia and England. But the duke and the chancellor held the secret, unknown to any one else - a locket. In a garret in Dresden the agents of Herbeck found her, a singer in the chorus of the opera. The newspapers and illustrated weeklies raged about her for a while, elaborated the story of her struggles, the mysterious remittances which had, from time to time, saved her from direst poverty, her ambition, her education which, by dint of hard work, she had acquired. It was all very puzzling and interesting and romantic. For what purpose had she been stolen, and by whom? The duke accused Franz of Jugendheit, but he did so privately. Search as they would, the duke and the chancellor never traced the source of the remittances. The duke held stubbornly that the sender of these benefactions was moved by the impulse of a guilty conscience, and that this guilty conscience was in Jugendheit. But these remittances, argued Herbeck, came long after the death of the old king. He had his agents, vowed the duke. Herbeck would not listen to this. He preferred to believe that Count von Arnsberg was the man.

There was an endless tangle of red tape before the girl

became secure in her rights. But finally, when William of Prussia and Franz Josef of Austria congratulated the duke, everybody else fell into line, and every troop in the duchy came to Dreiberg to the celebration. Then the world ran away in pursuit of other adventures, and forgot all about her serene highness.

And was she happy with all this grandeur, with all these lackeys and attentions and environs? Who can say? Sometimes she longed for the freedom and lack-care of her Dresden garret, her musician friends, the studios, the crash and glitter of the opera. To be suddenly deprived of the fruits of ambition, to reach such a pinnacle without striving, to be no longer independent, somehow it was all tasteless with the going of the novelty.

She looked like a princess, she moved and acted like one, but after the manner of kindly fairy princesses in story-books. All fell in love with her, from the groom who saddled her horse, to the chancellor, who up to this time was known never to have loved anything but the state.

She was lovely enough to inspire fervor and homage and love in all masculine minds. She was witty and talented. Carmichael said she was one of the most beautiful women in Europe. Later he modified this statement by declaring that she was the most beautiful woman in Europe or elsewhere. Yet, often she went about as one in a waking dream. There was an aloofness which was not born of hauteur but rather of a lingering doubt of herself.

She was still in the window-seat when the chancellor was announced. She distrusted him a little, she knew not why; yet, when he bent over her hand she was certain that his whole heart was behind his salute.

"Your Highness," he said, "I am come to announce to you that there waits for you a high place in the affairs of the world."

"The second crown in Jugendheit?"

"Your father - ?"

"Yes. He leaves the matter wholly in my hands."

The sparkle in his eyes was the first evidence of emotion she had ever seen in him. It rather pleased her.

"It is for the good of the state. A princess like yourself must never wed an inferior."

"Would a man who was brave and kind and resourceful, but without a title, would he be an inferior?"

"Assuredly, politically. And I regret to say that your marriage could never be else than a matter of politics."

"I am, then, for all that I am a princess, simply a certificate of exchange?"

His keen ear caught the bitter undercurrent. "The king of Jugendheit is young. I do not see how he can help loving you the moment he knows you. Who can?" And the chancellor enjoyed the luxury of a smile.

"But he may not be heart whole."

"He will be, politically."

"Politics, politics; how I hate the word! Sometimes I regret my garret."

The chancellor frowned. "Your Highness, I beg of you never to give that thought utterance in the presence of your father."

"Ah, believe me, I am not ungrateful; but all this is new to me, even yet. I am living in a dream, wondering and wondering when I shall wake."

The chancellor wrinkled his lips. It was more of a grimace than a smile.

"Will you consent to this marriage?"

"Would it do any good to reject it?"

"On the contrary, it would do Ehrenstein great harm."

"Give me a week," wearily.

"A week!" There was joy on the chancellor's face now, unmasked, unconcealed. "Oh, when the moment comes that I see the crown of Jugendheit on your beautiful head, all my work shall not have been in vain. So then, within seven days I shall come for your answer?"

"One way or the other, my answer will be ready then."

"There is one thing more, your Highness."

"And that?"

"There must not be so many rides in the morning with his excellency, Herr Carmichael."

She met his piercing glance with that mild duplicity known only to women. "He is a gentleman, he amuses me, and there is no harm. Grooms are always with us. And often he is only

Harold MacGrath

one of a party."

"It is politics again, your Highness; I merely offer the suggestion."

"Marry me to the king of Jugendheit, if you will, but in this I shall have my way." But she laughed as she laid down this law.

He surrendered his doubt. "Well, for a week. But once the banns are published, it will be neither wise nor - "

"Proper? That is a word, Count, that I do not like."

"Pardon me, your Highness. All this talk is merely for the sake of saving you needless embarrassment."

He bowed and took his leave of her.

"Jugendheit! Ah, I had rather my garret, my garret!"

And her gaze sped across the Platz and lingered about one of the little window-balconies of the Grand Hotel.

CHAPTER IV

THE YOUNG VINTNER

The Black Eagle (*Zum Schwartzen Adler*) in the Adlergasse was a prosperous tavern of the second rate. The house was two hundred years old and had been in the Bauer family all that time.

Had Fraeu Bauer, or Fraeu-Wirtin, as she was familiarly called, been masculine, she would have been lightly dubbed Bauer VII. She was a widow, and therefore uncrowned. She had been a widow for many a day, for the novelty of being her own manager had not yet worn off. She was thirty-eight, plump, pretty in a free-hand manner, and wise. It was useless to loll about the English bar where she kept the cash-drawer; it was useless to whisper sweet nothings into her ear; it was more than useless, it was foolish.

"Go along with you, Herr; I wouldn't marry the best man living. I can add the accounts, I can manage. Why should I marry?"

"But marriage is the natural state!"

"Herr, I crossed the frontier long ago, but having recrossed it, never again shall I go back. One crown-forty, if you please.

Thank you."

This retort had become almost a habit with the Fraeu-Wirtin; and when a day went by without a proposal, she went to bed with the sense that the day had not been wholly successful.

To-night the main room of the tavern swam in a blue haze of smoke, which rose to the blackened rafters, hung with many and various sausages, cheeses, and dried vegetables. Dishes clattered, there was a buzzing of voices, a scraping of feet and chairs, a banging of tankards, altogether noisy and cheerful. The Fraeu-Wirtin preferred waitresses, and this preference was shared by her patrons. They were quicker, cleaner; they remembered an order better; they were not always surreptitiously emptying the dregs of tankards on the way to the bar, as men invariably did. Besides, the barmaid was an English institution, and the Fraeu-Wirtin greatly admired that race, though no one knew why. The girls fully able to defend themselves, and were not at all diffident in boxing a smart fellow's ears. They had a rough wit and could give and take. If a man thought this an invitation and tried to take a kiss, he generally had his face slapped for his pains, and the Fraeu-Wirtin was always on the side of her girls.

The smoke was so thick one could scarcely see two tables away, and if any foreigner chanced to open a window there was a hubbub; windows were made for light, not air. There were soldiers, non-commissioned officers - for the fall maneuvers brought many to Dreiberg - farmers and their families, and the men of the locality who made the Black Eagle a kind of socialist club. Socialism was just taking hold in those days, and the men were tremendously serious and secretive regarding it, as it wasn't strong enough to be popular with governments which ruled by hereditary might and right.

Gretchen came in, a little better dressed than in the daytime, the change consisting of coarse stockings and shoes of leather, of which she was correspondingly proud.

"Will you want me, Fraeu-Wirtin, for a little while to-night?" she asked.

"Till nine. Half a crown as usual."

Gretchen sought the kitchen and found an apron and cap. These half-crowns were fine things to pick up occasionally, for it was only upon occasions that she worked at the Black Eagle.

In an obscure corner sat the young vintner. He had finished his supper and was watching and scrutinizing all who came in. His face brightened as he saw the goose-girl; he would have known that head anywhere, whether he saw the face or not. He wanted to go to her at once, but knew this action would not be wise.

In the very corner itself, his back to the vintner's, and nothing but the wall to look at, was the old man in tatters and patches, the mountaineer who possessed a Swiss watch and gave golden coins to goose-girls. He was busily engaged in gnawing the leg of a chicken. Between times he sipped his beer, listening.

Carmichael had forgotten some papers that day. He had dined early at the hotel and returned at once to the consulate. He was often a visitor at the Black Eagle. The beer was sweet and cool. So, having pocketed his papers, he was of a mind to carry on a bit of badinage with Fraeu Bauer. As he stepped into the big hall, in his evening clothes, he was as conspicuous as a passing ship at sea.

"Good evening, Fraeu-Wirtin."

"Good evening, your Excellency." She was quite fluttered when this fine young man spoke to her. He was the only person who ever caused her embarrassment, even though temporary. There was always a whimsical smile on his lips and in his eyes, and Fraeu Bauer never knew exactly how to take him. "What is on your mind?" brightly.

"Many things. You haven't aged the least since last I saw you."

"Which was day before yesterday!"

"Not any further back than that?"

"Not an hour."

She turned to make change, while Carmichael's eyes roved in search of a vacant chair. He saw but one.

"The goose-girl?" he murmured suddenly. "Is Gretchen one of your waitresses?"

"She comes in once in a while. She's a good girl and I'm glad to help her," Fraeu Bauer replied.

"I do not recollect having seen her here before."

"That is because you rarely come at night."

Gretchen carried a tray upon which steamed a vegetable stew. She saw Carmichael and nodded.

"I shall be at yonder table," he said indicating the vacant chair. "Will you bring me a tankard of brown Ehrensteiner?"

"At once, Herr."

Carmichael made his way to the table. Across the room he had not recognized the vintner, but now he remembered. He had crowded him against a wall two or three days before.

"This seat is not reserved, Herr?" he asked pleasantly, with his hand on the back of the chair.

"No." There was no cordiality in the answer. The vintner turned back the lid of his stein and drank slowly.

Carmichael sat down sidewise, viewing the scene with never-waning interest. These German taverns were the delight of his soul. Everybody was so kindly and orderly and hungry. They ate and drank like persons whose consciences were not overburdened. From the corner of his eye he observed that the vintner was studying him. Now this vintner's face was something familiar. Carmichael stirred his memory. It was not in Dreiberg that he had seen him before. But where?

Gretchen arrived with the tankard which she sat down at Carmichael's elbow.

"Will you not join me, Herr?" he invited.

"Thank you," said the vintner, without hesitation.

He smiled at Gretchen and she smiled at him. Carmichael smiled at them both tolerantly.

"What will you be drinking?"

"Brown," said the vintner.

Gretchen took up the empty tankard and made off. The eyes

Harold MacGrath

of the two men followed her till she reached the dim bar, then their glances swung round and met. Carmichael was first to speak, not because he was forced to, but because it was his fancy at that moment to give the vintner the best of it.

"She is a fine girl."

"Yes," tentatively.

"She is the handsomest peasant I ever saw or knew."

"You know her?" There was a spark in the vintner's eyes.

"Only for a few days. She interests me." Carmichael produced a pipe and lighted it.

"Ah, yes, the pretty peasant girl always interests you gentlemen." There was a note of bitterness. "Did you come here to seek her?"

"This is the first time I ever saw her here. And let me add," evenly, "that my interest in her is not of the order you would infer. She is good and patient and brave, and my interest in her is impersonal. It is not necessary for me to make any explanations, but I do so."

"Pardon me!" The vintner was plainly abashed.

"Granted. But you, you seem to possess a peculiar interest."

The vintner flushed. "I have that right," with an air which rather mystified Carmichael.

"That explains everything. I do not recollect seeing you before in the Black Eagle."

"I am from the north; a vintner, and there is plenty of work here in the valleys late in September."

"The grape," mused Carmichael. "You will never learn how to press it as they do in France. It is wine there; it is vinegar this side of the Rhine."

"France," said the vintner moodily. "Do you think there will be any France in the future?"

Carmichael laughed. "France is an incurable cosmic malady; it will always be. It may be beaten, devastated, throttled, but it will not die."

"You are fond of France?"

"Very."

"Do you think it wise to say so here?"

"I am the American consul; nobody minds my opinions."

"The American consul," repeated the vintner.

Gretchen could now be seen, wending her return in and out among the clustering tables. She set the tankards down, and Carmichael put out a silver crown.

"And do not bother about the change."

"Are all Americans rich?" she asked soberly. "Do you never keep the change yourselves?"

"Not when we are in our Sunday clothes."

"Then it is vanity." Gretchen shook her head wisely.

"Mine is worth only four coppers to-night," he said.

The vintner laughed pleasantly. Gretchen looked into his eyes, and an echo found haven in her own.

Carmichael thirstily drank his first tankard, thinking: "So this vintner is in love with our goose-girl? Confound my memory! It never failed me like this before. I would give twenty crowns to know where I have seen him. It's only the time and place that bothers me, not the face. A fine beer," he said aloud, holding up the second tankard.

The vintner raised his; there was an unconscious grace in the movement. A covert glance at his hand satisfied Carmichael in regard to one thing. He might be a vintner, but the hand was as soft and well-kept as a woman's, for all that it was stained by wind and sunshine. A handsome beggar, whoever and whatever he was. But a second thought disturbed him. Could a man with hands like these mean well toward Gretchen? He was a thorough man of the world; he knew innocence at first glance, and Gretchen was both innocent and unworldly. To the right man she might be easy prey. Never to a man like Colonel von Wallenstein, whose power and high office were alike sinister to any girl of the peasantry; but a man in the guise of her own class, of her own world and people, here was a snare Gretchen might not be able to foresee. He would watch this fellow, and at the first sign of an evil - Carmichael's muscular brown hands opened and shut ominously. The vintner did not observe this peculiar expression of the hands; and Carmichael's face was bland.

A tankard, rapping a table near-by, called Gretchen to her duties. There was something reluctant in her step, in the good-by glance, in the sudden fall of the smiling lips.

"She will make some man a good wife," said Carmichael.

The vintner scowled at his tankard.

"He is not sure of her," thought Carmichael. Aloud he said: "What a funny world it is!"

"How?"

"Gretchen is beautiful enough to be a queen, and yet she is merely a Hebe in a tavern."

"Hebe?" suspiciously. The peasant is always suspicious of anything he doesn't understand.

"Hebe was a cup-bearer to the mythological gods in olden times," Carmichael explained. He had set a trap, but the vintner had not fallen into it.

"A fairy-story." The vintner nodded; he understood now.

Carmichael's glance once more rested on the vintner's hand. He would lay another trap.

"What happened to her?"

"Oh," said Carmichael, "she spilled wine on a god one day, and they banished her."

"It must have been a rare vintage."

"I suppose you are familiar with all valleys. Moselle?"

"Yes. That is a fine country."

The old man in tatters sat erect in his chair, but he did not turn his head.

"You have served?"

"A little. If I could be an officer I should like the army." The vintner reached for his pipe which lay on the table.

"Try this," urged Carmichael, offering his pouch.

"This will be good tobacco, I know." The vintner filled his pipe.

Carmichael followed this gift with many questions about wines and vintages; and hidden in these questions were a dozen clever traps. But the other walked over them, unhesitant, with a certainty of step which chagrined the trapper.

By and by the vintner rose and bade his table-companion a good night. He had not offered to buy anything, another sign puzzling to Carmichael. This frugality was purely of the thrifty peasant. But the vintner was not ungrateful, and he expressed many thanks. On his way to the door he stopped, whispered into Gretchen's ear, and passed out into the black street.

"Either he is a fine actor, or he is really what he says he is." Carmichael was dissatisfied. "I'll stake my chances on being president of the United States, which is safe enough as a wager, that this fellow is not genuine. I'll watch him. I've stumbled upon a pretty romance of some sort, but I fear that it is one-sided." He wrinkled his forehead, but that part of his recollection he aimed to stir remained fallow, in darkness.

The press in the room was thinning. There were vacant chairs here and there now. A carter sauntered past and sat down unconcernedly at the table occupied by the old man whose face Carmichael had not yet seen. The two exchanged not even so much as a casual nod. A little later a butcher approached the same table and seated himself after the manner of the carter. It was only when the dusty baker came along and repeated this procedure, preserving the same silence, that Carmichael's curiosity was enlivened. This curiosity, however, was only of the evanescent order. Undoubtedly they were socialists and this was a little conclave, and the peculiar manner of their meeting, the silence and mystery, were purely fictional. Socialism at that time revolved round the blowing up of kings, of demolishing established order. Neither kings were blown up nor order demolished, but it was a congenial topic over which to while away an evening. This was in the German states; in Russia it was a different matter.

Had Carmichael not fallen a-dreaming over his pipe he would have seen the old man pass three slips of paper across the table; he would have seen the carter, the butcher, and the baker pocket these slips stolidly; he would have seen the mountaineer wave his hand sharply and the trio rise and disperse. And perhaps it would have been well for him to have noted these singular manifestations of conspiracy, since shortly he was to become somewhat involved. It was growing late; so Carmichael left the Black Eagle, nursing the sunken ember in his pipe and surrendering no part of his dream.

Intermediately the mountaineer paid his score and started for the stairs which led to the bedrooms above. But he stopped at the bar. A very old man was having a pail filled with hot cabbage soup. It was the ancient clock-mender across the way. The mountaineer was startled out of his habitual reserve, but he recovered his composure almost instantly. The clock-mender, his heavy glasses hanging crookedly on his nose, his whole aspect that of a weary, broken man, took down his pail and shuffled noiselessly out. The mountaineer followed him cautiously. Once in his shop the clock-mender poured the steaming soup into a bowl, broke bread in it, and began his evening meal. The other, his face pressed against the dim pane, stared and stared.

"*Gott in Himmel!* It is *he*!" he breathed, then stepped back into the shadow, while the moisture from his breath slowly faded and disappeared from the window-pane.

CHAPTER V

A COMPATRIOT

Krumerweg was indeed a crooked way. It formed a dozen elbows and ragged half-circles as it slunk off from the Adlergasse. Streets have character even as humans, and the Krumerweg reminded one of a person who was afraid of being followed. The shadow of the towering bergs lay upon it, and the few stars that peered down through the narrow crevice of rambling gables were small, as if the brilliant planets had neither time nor inclination to watch over such a place. And yet there lived in the Krumerweg many a kind and loyal heart, stricken with poverty. In old times the street had had an evil name, now it possessed only a pitiful one.

It was half after nine when Gretchen and the vintner picked their way over cobbles pitted here and there with mud-holes. They were arm in arm, and they laughed when they stumbled, laughed lightly, as youth always laughs when in love.

"Only a little farther," said Gretchen, for the vintner had never before passed over this way.

"Long as it is and crooked, Heaven knows it is short enough!" He encircled her with his arms and kissed her. "I love you! I love you!" he said.

Gretchen was penetrated with rapture, for her ears, sharp with love and the eternal doubting of man, knew that falsehood could not lurk in such music. This handsome boy loved her. Buffeted as she had been, she could separate the false from the true. Come never so deep a sorrow, there would always be this - he loved her. Her bosom swelled, her heart throbbed, and she breathed in ecstasy the sweet chill air that rushed through the broken street.

"After the vintage," she said, giving his arm a pressure. For this handsome fellow was to be her husband when the vines were pruned and freshened against the coming winter.

"Aye, after the vintage," he echoed; but there was tragedy in his heart as deep and profound as his love.

"My grandmother - I call her that for I haven't any grandmother - is old and seldom leaves the house. I promised that after work to-night I'd bring my man home and let her see how handsome he is. She is always saying that we need a man about; and yet, I can do a man's work as well as the next one. I love you, too, Leo!" She pulled his hand to her lips and quickly kissed it, frightened but unashamed.

"Gretchen, Gretchen!"

She stopped. "What is it?" keenly. "There was pain in your voice."

"The thought of how I love you hurts me. There is nothing else, nothing, neither riches nor crowns, nothing but you, Gretchen. How long ago was it I met you first?"

"Two weeks."

"Two weeks? Is it not years? Have I not always known and loved you?"

"And I! What an empty heart and head were mine till that wonderful day! You were tired and dusty and footsore; you had walked some twenty odd miles; yet you helped me with the geese. There were almost tears in your eyes, but I knew that your heart was a man's when you smiled at me." She stopped again and turned him round to her. "And you love me like this?"

"Whatever betide, *Lieberherz*, whatever befall." And he embraced her with a fierce tenderness, and so strong was he in the moment that Gretchen gave a cry. He kissed her, not on the lips, but on the fine white forehead, reverently.

They proceeded, Gretchen subdued and the vintner silent, until they came to the end of their journey at number forty in the Krumerweg. It was a house of hanging gables, almost as old as the town itself, solid and grim and taciturn. There are some houses which talk like gossips, noisy, obtrusive and provocative. Number forty was like an old warrior, gone to his chair by the fireside, who listens to the small-talk of his neighbors saturninely. What was it all about? Had he not seen battles and storms, revolutions and bloodshed? The prattle of children was preferable.

Gretchen's grandmother, Fraeu Schwarz, owned the house; it was all that barricaded her from poverty's wolves, and, what with sundry taxes and repairs and tenants who paid infrequently, it was little enough. Whatever luxuries entered at number forty were procured by Gretchen herself. At present the two stories were occupied; the second by a malter and his brood of children, the third by a woman who was partially bedridden. The lower or ground floor of four rooms she reserved for herself. As a matter of fact the forward room, with its huge middle-age fireplace and the great square of beamed and plastered walls and stone flooring, was sizable for all domestic purposes. Gretchen's pallet stood in a small alcove and the old woman's bed by the left of the fire.

Gretchen opened the door, which was unlocked. There was no light in the hall. She pressed her lover in her arms, kissed him lightly, and pushed him into the living-room. A log smoldered dimly on the irons. Gretchen ran forward, turned over the log, lighted two candles, then kissed the old woman seated in the one comfortable chair. The others were simply three-legged stools. There was little else in the room, save a poor reproduction of the Virgin Mary.

"Here I am, grandmother!"

"And who is here with you?" sharply but not unkindly.

"My man!" cried Gretchen gaily, her eyes bright as the candle flames.

"Bring him near me."

Gretchen gathered up two stools and placed them on either side of her grandmother and motioned to the vintner to sit down. He did so, easily and without visible embarrassment, even though the black eyes plunged a glance into his.

Her hair was white and thin, her nose aquiline, her lips fallen in, a cobweb of wrinkles round her eyes, down her cheeks, under her chin. But her sight was undimmed.

"Where are you from? You are not a Dreiberger."

"From the north, grandmother," forcing a smile to his lips.

The reply rather gratified her.

"Your name."

"Leopold Dietrich, a vintner by trade."

"You speak like a Hanoverian or a Prussian."

"I have passed some time in both countries. I have wandered about a good deal."

"Give me your hand."

The vintner looked surprised for a moment. Gretchen approved. So he gave the old woman his left hand. The grandmother smoothed it out upon her own and bent her shrewd eyes. Silence. Gretchen could hear the malter stirring above; the log cracked and burst into flame. A frown began to gather on the vintner's brow and a sweat in his palm.

"I see many strange things here," said the palmist, in a brooding tone.

"And what do you see?" asked Gretchen eagerly.

"I see very little of vineyards. I see riches, pomp; I see vast armies moving against each other; there is the smell of powder and fire; devastation. I do not see you, young man, among those who tramp with guns on their shoulders. You ride; there is gold on your arms. You will become great; but I do not understand. I do not understand," closing her eyes for a moment.

The vintner sat upright, his chin truculent, his arm tense.

"War!" he murmured.

Gretchen's heart sank; there was joy in his voice.

"Go on, grandmother," she whispered.

"Shall I live?" asked the vintner, whose belief in prescience till this hour had been of a negative quality.

"There is nothing here save death in old age, vintner." Her gnarled hand seized his in a vise. "Do you mean well by my girl?"

"Grandmother!" Gretchen remonstrated.

"Silence!"

The vintner withdrew his hand slowly.

"Is this the hand of a liar and a cheat? Is it the hand of a dishonest man?"

"There is no dishonesty there; but there are lines I do not understand. Oh, I can not see everything; it is like seeing people in a mist. They pass instantly and disappear. But I repeat, do you mean well by my girl?"

"Before God and His angels I love her; before all mankind I would gladly declare it. Gretchen shall never come to harm at these hands. I swear it."

"I believe you." The old woman's form relaxed its tenseness.

"Thanks, grandmother," said Gretchen. "Now, read what my hand says."

The old woman took the hand. She loved Gretchen.

"I read that you are gentle and brave and cheerful, that you have a loyal heart and a pure mind. I read that you are in love and that some day you will be happy." A smile went over her face, a kind of winter sunset.

"You are not looking at my hand at all, grandmother," said Gretchen in reproach.

"I do not need, my child. Your life is written in your face." The grandmother spoke again to the vintner. "So you will take her away from me?"

"Will it be necessary?" he returned quietly. "Have you any objection to my becoming your foster grandchild, such as Gretchen is?"

The old woman made no answer. She closed her eyes and did not open them. Gretchen motioned that this was a sign that the interview was ended. But as he rose to his feet there was a sound outside. A carriage had stopped. Some one opened the door and began to climb the stairs. The noise ceased only when the visitor reached the top landing. Then all became still again.

"There is something strange going on up there," said Gretchen in a whisper.

"In what way?" asked the vintner in like undertones.

"Three times a veiled lady has called at night, three times a man muffled up so one could not see his face."

"Let us not question our twenty-crowns rent, Gretchen," interrupted the grandmother, waking. "So long as no one is disturbed, so long as the police are not brought to our door, it is not our affair. Leopold, Gretchen, give me your hands."

She placed them one upon the other, then spread out her hands above their heads. "The Holy Mother bring happiness and good luck to you, Gretchen."

"And to me?" said the youth.

"I could not wish you better luck than to give you Gretchen. Now, leave me."

The vintner picked up his hat and Gretchen led him to the street.

He hurried away, giving no glance at the closed carriage, the sleepy driver, the weary horse. Neither did he heed the man dressed as a carter who, when he saw the vintner, turned and followed. Finally, when the vintner veered into the Adlergasse, he stopped, his hands clenched, his teeth hard upon each other. He even leaned against the wall of a house, his face for the moment hidden in his arm.

"Wretch that I am! Damnable wretch! Krumerweg, Krumerweg! Crooked way, indeed!" He flung down his arm passionately. "There will be a God up yonder," looking at the stars. "He will see into my heart and know that it is not bad, only young. Oh, Gretchen!"

"Gretchen?" The carter stepped into a shadow and waited.

* * * * *

Carmichael did not enjoy the opera that night. He had missed the first acts, and the last was gruesome, and the royal box was vacant. Outside he sat down on one of the benches near the fountains in the Platz. His prolific imagination took the boundaries. Ah! That morning's ride, down the southern path of the mountains, the black squirrels in the branches, the red fox in the bushes, the clear spring, and the drink out of the tin cup which hung there for the thirsty! How prettily she had wrapped a leaf over the rusted edge of the cup! The leaf lay in his pocket. He had kissed a dozen times the spot where her lips had pressed it. Blind fool! Deeper and deeper; he knew that he never could go back to that safe ledge of the heart-free. Time could not change his heart, not if given the thousand years of the wandering Jew.

Bah! He would walk round the fountain and cool his crazy pulse. He was Irish, Irish to the core. Would any one, save an Irishman, give way, day after day, to those insane maunderings? His mood was savage; he was at odds with the world, and most of all, with himself. If only some one would come along and shoulder him rudely! He laughed ruefully. He was in a fine mood to make an ass of himself.

He left the bench and strolled round the fountain, his cane behind his back, his chin in his collar. He had made the circle several times, then he blundered into some one. The fighting mood was gone now, the walk having calmed him. He murmured a short apology for his clumsiness and started on, without even looking at the animated obstacle.

"Just a moment, my studious friend."

"Wallenstein? I didn't see you." Carmichael halted.

"That was evident," replied the colonel jestingly. "Heavens! Have you really cares of state, that you walk five times round this fountain, bump into me, and start to go on without so much as a how-do-you-do?"

"I'm absent-minded," Carmichael admitted.

"Not always, my friend."

"No, not always. You have some other meaning?"

"That is possible. Now, I do not believe that it was absent-mindedness which made you step in between me and that pretty goose-girl, the other night."

"Ah!" Carmichael was all alertness.

"It was not, I believe?"

"It was coldly premeditated," said Carmichael, folding his arms over his cane which he still held behind his back. His attitude and voice were pleasant.

"It was not friendly."

"Not to you, perhaps. But that happens to be an innocent girl, Colonel. You're no Herod. There was nothing selfish in my act. You really annoyed her."

"Pretense; they always begin that way."

"I confess I know little about that kind of hunting, but I'm sure you've started the wrong quarry this time."

"You are positive that you were disinterested?"

"Come, come, Colonel, this sounds like the beginning of a quarrel; and a quarrel should never come into life between you and me. I taught you draw-poker; you ought to be grateful for that, and to accept my word regarding my disinterestedness."

"I do not wish any quarrel, my Captain; but that girl's face has fascinated me. I propose to see her as often as I like."

"I have no objection to offer; but I told Gretchen that if any one, no matter who, ever offers her disrespect, to report the matter to me at the consulate."

"That is meddling."

"Call it what you like, my Colonel."

"Well, in case she is what you consider insulted, what will you do?" a challenge in his tones.

"Report the matter to the police."

Wallenstein laughed.

"And if the girl finds no redress there," tranquilly, "to the chancellor."

"You would go so far?"

"Even further," unruffled.

"It looks as though you had drawn your saber," with irony.

"Oh, I can draw it, Colonel, and when I do I guarantee you'll find no rust on it. Come," and Carmichael held out his hand amicably, "Gretchen is already in love with one of her kind. Let the child be in peace. What! Is not the new ballerina enough conquest? They are all talking about it."

"Good night, Herr Carmichael!" The colonel, ignoring the friendly hand, saluted stiffly, wheeled abruptly, and left Carmichael staring rather stupidly at his empty hand.

"Well, I'm hanged! All right," with a tilt of the shoulders. "One enemy more or less doesn't matter. I'm not afraid of anything save this fool heart of mine. If he says an ill word to Gretchen, and I hear of it, I'll cane the blackguard, for that's what he is at bottom. Well, I was looking for trouble, and here it is, sure enough."

He saw a carriage coming along. He recognized the white horse as it passed the lamps. He stood still for a space, undecided. Then he sped rapidly toward the side gates of the royal gardens. The vehicle stopped there. But this time no woman came out. Carmichael would have recognized that lank form anywhere. It was the chancellor. Well, what of it? Couldn't the chancellor go out in a common hack if he wanted to? But who was the lady in the veil?

"I've an idea!"

As soon as the chancellor disappeared, Carmichael hailed the coachman.

"Drive me through the gardens."

"It is too late, Herr."

"Well, drive me up and down the Strasse while I finish this cigar."

"Two crowns."

"Three, if your horse behaves well."

"He's as gentle as a lamb, Herr."

"And doubtless will be served as one before long. Can't you throw back the top?"

"In one minute!" Five crowns and three made eight crowns;

not a bad business these dull times.

Carmichael lolled in the worn cushions, wondering whether or not to question his man. But it was so unusual for a person of such particular habits as the chancellor to ride in an ordinary carriage. Carmichael slid over to the forward seat and touched the jehu on the back.

"Where did you take the chancellor to-night?" he asked.

"*Du lieber Gott!* Was that his excellency? He said he was the chief steward."

"So he is, my friend. I was only jesting. Where did you take him?"

"I took him to the Krumerweg. He was there half an hour. Number forty."

"Where did you take the veiled lady?"

The coachman drew in suddenly and apprehensively. "Herr, are you from the police?"

"Thousand thunders, no! It was by accident that I stood near the gate when she got out. Who was she?"

"That is better. They both told me that they were giving charity. I did not see the lady's face, but she went into number forty, the same as the steward. You won't forget the extra crown, Herr?"

"No; I'll make it five. Turn back and leave me at the Grand Hotel." Then he muttered: "Krumerweg, crooked way, number forty. If I see this old side-paddler stopping at the palace steps again, I'll take a look at number forty myself."

On the return to the hotel the station omnibus had arrived with a solitary guest. A steamer trunk and a couple of bags were being trundled in by the porter, while the concierge was helping a short, stocky man to the ground. He hurried into the hotel, signed the police slips, and asked for his room. He seemed to be afraid of the dark. He was gone when Carmichael went into the office.

"Your Excellency," said the concierge, rubbing his hands and smiling after the manner of concierges born in Switzerland, "a compatriot of yours arrived this evening."

"What name?" indifferently. Compatriots were always asking impossible things of Carmichael, introductions to the grand duke, invitations to balls, and so forth, and swearing to have him recalled if he refused to perform these offices.

The concierge picked up the slips which were to be forwarded to the police.

"He is Hans Grumbach, of New York."

"An adopted compatriot, it would seem. He'll probably be over to the consulate to-morrow to have his passports looked into. Good night."

So Hans Grumbach passed out of his mind; but for all that, fortune and opportunity were about to knock on Carmichael's door. For there was a great place in history ready for Hans Grumbach.

CHAPTER VI

AT THE BLACK EAGLE

The day promised to be mild. There was not a cloud anywhere, and the morning mists had risen from the valleys. It was good to stand in the sunshine which seemed to draw forth all the vagaries and weariness of sleep from the mind and body. Hans Grumbach shook himself gratefully. He was standing on the curb in front of the Grand Hotel, his back to the sun. It was nine o'clock. The broad Koenig Strasse shone, the white stone of the palaces glared, the fountains glistened, and the coloring tree tops scintillated like the head-dress of an Indian prince. Hans was short but strongly built; a mild blue-eyed German, smooth-faced, ruddy-cheeked, white-haired, with a brown button of a nose. He drank his beer with the best of them, but it never got so far as his nose save from the outside. His suit was tight-fitting, but the checks were ample, and the watch-chain a little too heavy, and the huge garnet on his third finger was not in good taste. But what's the odds? Grumbach was satisfied, and it's one's own satisfaction that counts most.

Presently two police officers came along and went into the hotel. Grumbach turned with a sigh and followed them. Doubtless they had come to look over his passports. And this happened to be the case.

Harold MacGrath

The senior officer unfolded the precious document.

"It is not yet viseed by your consul," said the officer.

"I arrived late last night. I shall see him this morning," replied Grumbach.

"You were not born in America?"

"Oh, no; I came from Bavaria."

"At what age?"

"I was twenty."

"Did you go to America with your parents?"

"No. I was alone."

"You still have your permit to leave Bavaria?"

"I believe so; I am not certain. I never thought in those days I should become rich enough to travel."

The word that tingled with gold soothed the suspicious ear of the officer.

"What is your business in America?"

"I am a plumber, now retired."

"And your business here?"

"Simply pleasure."

"You are forty?" said the officer, referring to the passports.

"Yes."

"This is rather young to retire from business."

"Not in America," easily.

"True, everybody grows rich there, with gold mines popping open at one's feet. It must be a great country." The officer sighed as he refolded the documents. "As soon as these are approved by his excellency the American consul, kindly have a porter bring them over to the bureau of police. It will be only a matter of form. I shall return them at once."

Grumbach produced a Louis Napoleon which was then as now acceptable that side of the Rhine. It was not done with pomposity, but rather with the exuberance of a man whose purse and letter of credit possess an assuring circumference.

"Drink a bottle, you and your comrade," he said.

This the officer promised to do forthwith. He returned the passports, put a hand to his cap respectfully and, followed by his assistant, walked off briskly.

Grumbach took off his derby and wiped the perspiration from his forehead. This moisture had not been wrung forth by any atmospheric effect. From the top of his forehead to the cowlick on the back of his head ran a broad white scar. At one time or another Grumbach had been on the ragged edge of the long journey. He went out of doors. There is nothing like sunshine to tonic the ebbing courage.

Coming up the thoroughfare, with a dash of spirit and color, was a small troop of horses. The sunlight broke upon the steel and silver. A waiter, cleaning off the little iron tables on the sidewalk, paused. The riders passed, all but two in splendid uniforms. Grumbach watched them till they disappeared into the palace courtyard. He called to the waiter.

"Who are they?"

"The grand duke and some of his staff, Herr."

"The grand duke? Who was the gentleman in civilian clothes?"

"That was his excellency, Herr Carmichael, the American consul."

"Very good. And the young lady?"

"Her serene highness, the Princess Hildegarde."

"Bring me a glass of beer," said Grumbach, sinking down at a table. A thousand questions surged against his lips, but he kept them shut with all the stolidity of his native blood. When the waiter set the beer down before him, he said: "Where does Herr Carmichael live?"

"The consulate is in the Adlergasse. He himself lives here at the Grand Hotel. *Ach*! He is a great man, Herr Carmichael."

"So?"

"A friend of the grand duke, a friend of her serene highness, liked everywhere, a fine shot and a great fencer, and rides a horse as if he were sewn to the saddle. And all the ladies admire him because he dances."

"So he dances? Quite a lady's man." To Grumbach a man who danced was a lady's man, something to be held in contempt.

"You would not call him a lady's man, if you mean he wastes his time on them."

"But you say he dances?"

"*Ach, Gott!* Don't we all dance to some tune or other?" cried the waiter philosophically.

"You are right; different music, different jigs. Take the coppers."

"Thanks, Herr." The waiter continued his work.

So Herr Carmichael lived here. That would be convenient. Grumbach decided to wait for him. He had seen enough of men to know if he could trust the consul. He glared at the amber-gold in the glass, took a vigorous swallow, and smacked his lips. A sentimental old fool; he was neither more nor less.

The wait for Carmichael was short. The American consul came along with energetic stride. He had been to the earlier maneuvers, and aside from coffee and bacon he had had no breakfast. The ride and the cold air of morning had made him ravenous. Grumbach rose and caught Carmichael by the arm.

"Your pardon, sir," he said in good English, "but you are Mr. Carmichael, the American consul?"

"I am."

"Will you kindly look over my papers?" Grumbach asked.

"You are from the United States?" Then Carmichael remembered that this must be the compatriot who arrived the night before. "I shall be very glad to see you in the Adlergasse at half after ten. It is one flight up, next door to the Black Eagle. Any one will show you the way. I haven't breakfasted yet, and I can not transact any business in these dusty clothes. Good morning."

Grumbach liked the consul's smile. More than that, he recognized instantly that this handsome young man was a gentleman. The inherent respect for caste had not been beaten out of Grumbach's blood; he had come from a brood in a peasant's hovel. To him the word gentleman would always signify birth and good clothes; what the heart and mind were did not matter much.

He had more than an hour to idle away, so he wandered through the park, admiring the freshness of the green, the well-kept flower-beds, the crisp hedges, and the clean graveled paths. There was nothing like it back there in America. They hadn't the time there; everybody was in the market, speculating in bubbles. He admired the snowy fountains, too, and the doves that darted in and out of the wind-blown spray. There was nothing like this in America, either. He was not belittling; he was only making comparisons. He knew that he would be far happier in his adopted country, which would accomplish all these beautiful things farther on.

He looked up heavenward, where the three bergs shouldered the dazzling snow into the blue. This impressed him more than all else; that little wrinkle in the middle berg's ice had been there when he was a boy. Nothing had changed in Dreiberg save the Koenig Strasse, whose cobbles had been replaced by smooth blocks of wood. At times he sent swift but uncertain glances toward the palaces. He longed to peer through the great iron fence, but he smothered this desire. He would find out what he wanted to know when he met

Carmichael at the consulate. Here the bell in the cathedral struck the tenth hour; not a semitone had this voice of bronze changed in all these years. It was good to be here in Dreiberg again. Should he ask the way to the Adlergasse? Perhaps this would be wiser. So he put the question to a policeman. The officer politely gave him a detailed route.

"Follow these directions and you will have no trouble in finding the Adlergasse."

"Much obliged."

Trouble? Scarcely! He had put out his first protest against the world in the Adlergasse, forty years since. He came to a stand before the old tavern. Not even the sign had been painted anew, though the oak board was a trifle paler and there was a little more rust on the hinges. Many a time he had fought with the various pot-boys. He wondered if there were any pot-boys inside now. He noted the dingy consulate sign, then started up the dark and narrow stairs. The consulate door stood open.

A clerk, native to Ehrenstein, was writing at a table. At a desk by the window sat Carmichael, deep in a volume of Dumas. No one ever hurried here; no one ever had palpitation of the heart over business. The clerk lifted his head.

"Mr. Carmichael?" said Grumbach in English.

The clerk indicated with his pen toward the individual by the window. Carmichael read on. Grumbach had assimilated some Americanisms. He went boldly over and seated himself in the chair at the side of the desk. With a sigh Carmichael left Porthos in the grotto of Locmaria.

"I am Mr. Grumbach. I spoke to you this morning about my

passports. Will you kindly look them over?"

Carmichael took the papers, frowning slightly. Grumbach laid his derby on his knees. The consul went over the papers, viseed them, and handed them to their owner.

"You will have no trouble going about with those," Carmichael said listlessly. "How long will you be in Dreiberg?"

"I do not know," said Grumbach truthfully.

"Is there anything I can do for you?"

"There is only one thing," answered Grumbach, "but you may object, and I shall not blame you if you do. It will be a great favor."

"What do you wish?" more listlessly.

"An invitation to the military ball at the palace, after the maneuvers," quietly.

Carmichael sat up. He had not expected so large an order as this.

"I am afraid you are asking something impossible for me to obtain," he replied coldly, thumbing the leaves of his book.

"Ah, Mr. Carmichael, it is very important that I should be there."

"Explain."

"I can give you no explanations. I wish to attend this ball. I do not care to meet the grand duke or any one else. Put me in the gallery where I shall not be noticed. That is all I ask of you."

"That might be done. But you have roused my curiosity. Your request is out of the ordinary. You have some purpose?"

"A perfectly harmless one," said Grumbach, mopping his forehead.

This movement brought Carmichael's eye to the scar. Grumbach acknowledged the stare by running his finger along the subject.

"I came near passing in my checks the day I got that," he volunteered. "Everybody looks at it when I take off my hat. I've tried tonics, but the hair won't grow there."

"Where did you get it?"

"At Gettysburg."

"Gettysburg?" with a lively facial change. "You were in the war?"

"All through it."

Carmichael was no longer indifferent. He gave his hand.

"I've got a few scars myself. What regiment?"

"The - th cavalry, New York."

"What troop?" with growing excitement.

"C troop."

"I was captain of B troop in the same regiment. Hurrah! Work's over for the day. Come along with me, Grumbach, and we'll talk it over down-stairs in the Black Eagle. You're a godsend. C troop! Hanged if the world doesn't move things about oddly. I was in the hospital myself after Gettysburg; a ball in the leg. And I've rheumatism even now when a damp spell comes."

So down to the tavern they went, and there they talked the battles over, sundry tankards interpolating. It was "Do you remember this?" and, "Do you recall that?" with diagrams drawn in beer on the oaken table.

"But there's one thing, my boy," said Carmichael.

"What's that?"

"The odds were on our side, or we'd be fighting yet."

"That we would. The poor devils were always hungry when we whipped them badly."

"But you're from this side of the water?"

"Yes; went over when I was twenty-two." Grumbach sucked his pipe stolidly.

"What part of Germany?"

"Bavaria; it is so written in my passports."

"Munich?"

Grumbach circled the room. All the near tables were vacant. The Black Eagle was generally a lonely place till late in the afternoon. Grumbach touched the scar tenderly. Could he trust this man? Could he trust any one in the world? The impulse came to trust Carmichael, and he did not disregard it.

"I was born in this very street," he whispered.

"Here?"

"Sh! Not so loud! Yes, in this very street. But if the police knew, I wouldn't be worth *that!*" - with a snap of the fingers. "My passports, my American citizenship, they would be worthless. You know that."

"But what does this all mean? What have you done that you can't come back here openly?" Here was a mystery. This man with the kindly face and frank eyes could be no ordinary criminal. "Can I help you in any way?"

"No; no one can help me."

"But why did you come back? You were safe enough in New York."

"Who can say what a man will do? Don't question me. Let be. I have said too much already. Some day perhaps I shall tell you why. When I went away I was thin and pale and had yellow hair. To-day I am fat, gray-headed; I have made money. Who will recognize me now? No one."

"But your name?"

Grumbach laughed unmusically. "Grumbach is as good as another. Listen. You are my comrade now; we have shed our blood on the same field. There is no tie stronger than that. When I left Dreiberg there was a reward of a thousand crowns for me. Dead or alive, preferably dead."

Carmichael was plainly bewildered. He tried to recall the past history of Ehrenstein which would offer a niche for this inoffensive-looking German. He was blocked.

"Dead or alive," he repeated.

"So."

"You were mad to return."

"I know it. But I had to come; I couldn't help it. Oh, don't look like that! I never hurt anybody, unless it was in battle" - naively. "Ask no more, my friend. I promise to tell you when the right time comes. Now, will you get me that invitation to the gallery at the military ball?"

"I will, if you will give me your word, as a soldier, as a comrade in arms, that you have no other purpose than to look at the people."

"As God is my judge" - solemnly - "that is all I wish to do. Now, what has happened since I went away? I have dared to ask questions of no one."

Carmichael gave him a brief summary of events, principal among which was the amazing restoration of the Princess Hildegarde. When he had finished, Grumbach remained dumb and motionless for a time.

"And what is her serene highness like?"

To describe the Princess Hildegarde was not only an easy task, but a pleasant one to Carmichael, and if he embroidered this description here and there, Grumbach was too deeply concerned with the essential points to notice these variations in the theme.

"So she is gentle and beautiful? Why not? *Ach*! You should have seen her mother. She was the most beautiful woman in all Germany, and she sang like one of those Italian nightingales. I recall her when I was a boy. I would gladly have died at a word from her. All loved her. The king of Jugendheit wanted her, but she loved the grand duke. So the Princess Hildegarde has come back to her own? God is good!" And Grumbach bent his head reverently.

"Well," said Carmichael, beckoning to the waitress, and paying the score, "if any trouble rises, send for me. You don't look like a man who has done anything very bad." He offered his hand again.

Grumbach pressed it firmly, and there was a moisture in his eyes.

Together they returned to the Grand Hotel for lunch. On the way neither talked very much. They were both thinking of the same thing, but from avenues diametrically opposed. Grumbach declined Carmichael's invitation to lunch, and immediately sought his own room.

Once there, he closed the shutters so as to admit but half the day's light, and opened his battered trunk. From the false bottom, which had successfully eluded the vigilance of a dozen frontiers, he took out a small bundle. This he opened carefully, his eyes blurring. Mad fool that he had been! How many times had he gazed at these trinkets in these sixteen or more years? How often had he uttered lamentations over them? How many times had the talons of remorse gashed his heart?

Two little yellow shoes, so small that they lay on his palm as lightly as two butterflies; a little cloak trimmed with ermine; a golden locket shaped like a heart!

CHAPTER VII

AN ELDER BROTHER

Grumbach was very fond of music, and in America there were never any bands except at political meetings or at the head of processions; and that wasn't the sort of music he preferred. There was nothing at the Opera, so he decided to spend the earlier part of the evening in the public gardens. He was lonely; he had always been lonely. Men who carry depressing secrets generally are. He searched covertly among the many faces for one that was familiar, but he saw none; and he was at once glad, and sorry. Yes, there was one face; the rubicund countenance of the bandmaster. It was older, more wrinkled, but it was the same. How many years had the old fellow swung the baton? At least thirty years. In his boyhood days Grumbach had put that brilliant uniform side by side with the grand duke's. As it was impossible for him ever to become a duke, his ambition had been to arrive at the next greatest thing - the bandmaster. As he neared the pavilion he laughed silently and grimly. To have grown wealthy as a master plumber instead! So much for ambition!

Subsequently he found himself standing beside a young vintner and his peasant sweetheart. Their hands secretly met and locked behind their backs. Grumbach sighed. Never would he know aught of this double love. This Eden would never have any gate for him to push aside. He would always go his way alone.

The girl turned her head. Seeing Grumbach, she loosened the vintner's hand.

"Do not mind me, girl," said Grumbach, his face broadening.

The girl laughed easily and without confusion. Her companion, however, flushed under his tan, and a scowl ran over his forehead.

The band struck up, and the little comedy was forgotten. But Grumbach could not see anything except the girl's face, the fresh, exquisite turn of her profile. Once his eye wandered rather guiltily. Her figure was in keeping with her face. Then he saw the little wooden shoes. Ah, well, as long as kings surrounded themselves with armies and with pomp, there would always be wooden shoes. The band was playing *Les Huguenots*, and the girl hummed the air.

"Do not go there to-night, Gretchen," said the vintner.

"It is a crown."

"I will give you two if you will not go," the vintner urged.

"Foolish boy, what good would that do? We need every crown we have or can get, if we are to be married soon. And you have not gone to work yet. And every day costs you a crown to live, and more, for all I know. You spend a crown as carelessly as if all you had to do was to pick them off the vines. Crowns are hard to get."

"When one is happy, one does not stop to bother about crowns," he said impatiently.

"But will such happiness last? Shall we not be happier as our crowns accumulate, to ward off sickness and hunger? Must I teach you economy?"

"I shall apply for work to-morrow and waste no more crowns, my heart." The vintner's hand again sought hers, and he sent Grumbach a look which said: "Smile if you dare!"

But Grumbach did not smile. He was too sad. He fell into a dream, and the music faded in his ear and the lights of the pavilion grew dim. He was a boy again, and he was carrying posies to the pretty little fraeulein in the Adlergasse. Dreams never last, and sometimes they are rudely interrupted.

A hand was put upon his shoulder authoritatively. The police officer who had examined his passports that morning stood at Grumbach's elbow.

"Herr Grumbach," he said quietly, "his excellency the chancellor has directed me to bring you at once to the palace."

"To the palace?" Grumbach's face was expressive of great astonishment. The officer saw nothing out of the ordinary in this expression. Any foreigner would have been seized with confusion under like circumstances. "To the palace?" Grumbach repeated. "My passports were wrong in some respect?"

"Oh, no, Herr; they were correct."

Grumbach roused his mind energetically. He forced down the fast beating of his heart, banished the astonishment from his face, and even brought a smile to his lips.

"But whatever can the chancellor want of me?"

"That is not my business. I was simply sent to find you. His excellency is always interested in German-Americans. It may be that he wishes to ask what the future is there in America. We have more in Dreiberg than we can reasonably take care of."

"In the prisons?"

The officer laughed. "There and elsewhere."

"Is that right?" asked Grumbach, now thoroughly on guard.

"It may not be right to ship our criminals over there, but it is considered very good politics."

"Shall we go at once? I never expected to enter the palace of the grand duke of Ehrenstein," Grumbach added. "It will be something to tell of when I go back to America."

The only thing that reassured him was the presence of one officer. When they came for a man on a serious charge, in Ehrenstein, they came in pairs or fours. So then, there could be pending nothing vital to his liberty or his incognito. Besides, his papers were all right, and now there would be Carmichael to fall back on.

"The palace is lighted up," was Grumbach's comment as the two passed the sentry outside the gates.

"The duke gives the dinner to the diplomatic corps to-night."

"A fine thing to be a diplomat."

"I myself prefer fighting in the open. Diplomats? Their very precious hides are never anywhere near the wars they bring about. No, no; this way. We go in at the side."

"You'll have to guide me. Yes, these diplomats. Men like you and me do all the work. I was in the Civil War in America."

"That was a great fight," remarked the officer. "I should like to have been there."

"Four years; pretty long. Do you know Herr Carmichael?"

"The American consul? Oh, yes."

"He and I fought in the same regiment."

"Then you saw some pretty battles."

Grumbach took off his hat. "See that?"

"*Gott*! That must have been an ugly one."

"Almost crossed over when I got it. Is this the door?"

"Yes. I'll put you in snugly. You will probably have to wait for his excellency. But you'll have me for company till he appears."

Grumbach entered the palace with a brave heart and a steady mind.

* * * * *

The grand duke had a warm place in his heart for the diplomatic corps. He liked to see them gathered round his table, their uniforms glittering with orders and decorations. It was always a night of wits; and he sprang a hundred traps for comedy's sake, but these astonishing linguists seldom if ever blundered into one of them. They were eternally vigilant. It was no trifling matter to swing the thought from German into French or Italian or Hungarian; but they were seasoned veterans in the game, all save Carmichael, who spoke only French and German fluently. The duke, however, never tried needlessly to embarrass him. He admired Carmichael's mental agility. Never he thrust so keenly that the American was found lacking in an effective though simple parry.

"Your highness must recollect that I am not familiar with that tongue."

"Pardon me, Herr Captain!"

But there was always a twinkle in the ducal eye and an answering smile in the consul's.

The somber black of Carmichael's evening dress stood out conspicuously among the blue and green and red uniforms. Etiquette compelled him to wear silk stockings, but that was the single concession on his part. He wore no orders. An order of the third or fourth class held no allurement. Nothing less than the Golden Fleece would have interested him, and the grand duke himself could not boast of this rare and distinguished order. In truth, Carmichael coveted nothing but a medal for valor, and his own country had not yet come to recognize the usefulness of such a distinction.

All round him sat ministers or ambassadors; he alone represented a consulate. So his place at the table was honorary rather than diplomatic. It was his lively humorous personality the grand duke admired, not his representations.

The duke sat at the head of the table and her serene highness at the foot; and it was by the force of his brilliant wit that the princess did not hold in perpetuity the court at her end of the table. For a German princess of that time she was highly accomplished; she was ardent, whimsical, with a flashing mentality which rounded out and perfected her physical loveliness. Above and beyond all this, she had suffered, she had felt the pangs of poverty, the smart of unrecognized merit; she had been one of the people, and her sympathies would always be with them, for she knew what those about her only vaguely knew, the patience, the unmurmuring bravery of the poor. Never would she become sated with power so long as it gave her the right to aid the people. Never a new tax was levied that she did not lighten it in some manner; never an oppressive law was promulgated that she did not soften its severity. And so the populace loved her, for it did not take the people long to find out what she was trying to do for them. And perhaps they loved her because she had lived the greater part of her young life as one of them.

To-night there was love in the duke's eyes as he looked down the table's length; there was love in the old chancellor's eyes, too; and in Carmichael's. And there was love in her eyes as she gazed back at the two old men. But who could read her eyes whenever they roved in Carmichael's direction? Not even Gretchen's grandmother, who lived in the Krumerweg.

"Gentlemen," said the duke, rising and holding up his glass, "this night I give you a toast which I believe will be agreeable to all of you, especially to his excellency, Baron von Steinbock of Jugendheit. What is past is past; a new regime begins this night." He paused. All eyes were focused upon him in wonder. Only Baron von Steinbock displayed no more than ordinary interest. "I give you," resumed the duke, "her serene highness and his majesty, Frederick of Jugendheit!"

The princess grew delicately pale as the men and women sprang to their feet. Every hand swept toward her, holding a glass. She had surrendered that morning. Not because she wished to be a queen, not because she cared to bring about an alliance between the two countries; no, it was because she was afraid and had burned the bridge behind her.

The tan thinned on Carmichael's face, but his hand was steady. Never would he forget the tableau. She sat still in her chair, her lids drooped, but a proud lift to her chin. The collar of pearls round her neck had scarce more luster than her shoulders. How red her lips seemed against the whiteness of her skin! Beautiful to him beyond all dreams of beauty. God send another war and let him die in the heart of it, fighting! To dream lies as he had done this twelvemonth, to break his heart over the moon! He sat his glass down untouched, happily unobserved. He was in misery; he wanted to be alone.

"Long live her majesty!" thundered the chancellor. He, too, was pale, but the fire of great things burned in his eyes and his lank form took upon itself a transient majesty.

In the ball-room the princess was surrounded; everybody flattered her; congratulated her, and complimented her. All agreed that it was a great political stroke. And indeed it was, but none of them knew how great.

Carmichael was among the last to approach her. By this time he had his voice and nerves under control. Without apparent volition they walked down the stairs which led to the conservatory.

"I thought perhaps you had forgotten me," she said.

"Forget your highness? Do not give me credit for such an impossibility." He bowed over her hand and brushed it with his lips, for she was almost royal now. "Your highness will be happy. It is written." He stepped back slowly.

"Have you the gift of prescience?"

"In this instance. You will be a great queen."

"Who knows?" dreamily. "When I recall what I have gone through, all this seems like an enchantment out of a fairy-book, and that I must soon wake up in my garret in Dresden."

If only it might be an enchantment! he thought. If only he might find her as the grim old chancellor had found her, in a garret! What?

"Why did you do that?" she asked quickly.

"I do not understand."

"You shrugged."

"I beg your highness' pardon!" flushing. "I was not conscious of such rudeness."

"That is not answering my question."

"I beg of your highness - "

"My highness commands!" But her voice was gentle.

"It was a momentary dream I had; and the thought of its utter impossibility caused me to shrug. I assure your highness that it was a philosophical shrug, such as the Stoics were wont to indulge in." He spoke lightly. Only his eyes were serious.

"And this dream; was there not a woman in it?"

"Oh, no; there was only an angel."

She knew that it was not proper to question him in this manner; but neither her heart nor her mind were formal to-night.

"You interest me; you always interest me. You have seen so many wonderful things. And now it is angels."

"Only one, your Highness." This was daring. "But perhaps I am putting my foot where angels fear to tread," which was still more daring.

"Angels ought not to be afraid of anything." She laughed; there was a pain and a joy in the sound of it. She read his heart as one might read a written line.

"Dreams are always unfinished things," he said, getting back on safer ground.

"What is she like, this angel?" forcing him upon dangerous ground again wilfully.

"Who may describe an angel one has seen only in a golden dream?"

"You will not tell me?"

"I dare not!" His eyes sought hers unflinchingly. This moment he was mad, and had not the chancellor and Baron von Steinbock come up, Heaven only knew what further madness would have unbridled his tongue.

"Your Highness," began the benign voice of the chancellor, "the baron desires, in the name of his august master, to open the ball with you. Behold my fairy-wand," gaily. "This night

I have made you a queen."

"Can you make me happy also?" said she, so low that only the chancellor heard her.

"I shall try. Ah, Herr Captain," with a friendly jerk of his head toward Carmichael; "will you do me the honor to join me in my cabinet, quarter of an hour hence?"

"I shall be there, your Excellency." Carmichael was uneasy. He was not certain how much the chancellor had heard.

"A little diplomatic business in which I shall need your assistance," supplemented the chancellor.

Carmichael, instead of loitering uselessly in the ball-room, at once sought the chancellor's cabinet. He wanted to be alone. He made known his business to the chancellor's valet who admitted him. He stopped just across the threshold. To his surprise the room was already tenanted. Grumbach and a police officer!

"Why, Grumbach, what are you doing here?" cried Carmichael.

"Waiting for his excellency. We have been here something past an hour."

"What's the trouble?" Carmichael inquired.

"Your excellency knows as much as I do," said the officer, who was in fact no less than the sub-chief of the bureau.

"And I am in the dark, also," said Grumbach, twirling his hat.

Carmichael walked about, studying the many curios. Occasionally Grumbach wiped his forehead, and, absently, the inner rim of his hat. Perhaps the three of them waited twenty minutes; then the chancellor came in. He bowed cordially and drew chairs about his desk. He placed Grumbach in the full glare of the lamp. Carmichael and the sub-chief were in the half-light. The chancellor was last to seat himself.

"Herr Grumbach," said the chancellor in a mild tone, "I should like to see your papers."

"My passports, your Excellency?"

"Yes."

Grumbach laid them on the desk imperturbably. The chancellor struck the bell. His valet answered immediately.

"Send Breunner, the head gardener, at once."

"He is in the anteroom, Excellency."

"Tell him to come in."

The chancellor shot a piercing glance at Grumbach, but the latter was studying the mural decorations.

Carmichael sat tight in his chair, curious to learn what it was all about. Breunner entered. He was thin and partly bald and quite fifty.

"Breunner, her highness will need many flowers to-morrow. See to it that they are cut in the morning."

"It shall be done, Excellency."

The chancellor turned to the passports.

"There is only one question, Herr Grumbach. It says here that you were a native of Bavaria before going to America. How long ago did you leave Bavaria?"

"A good many years, your Excellency." Grumbach inspected the label in his hat.

"You have, of course, retained your Bavarian passport?"

Carmichael was now leaning forward in his chair, deeply interested. He saw that the chancellor was watching Grumbach as a cat watches a mouse-hole.

Grumbach brought forth a bulky wallet. The edges of Bank of England notes could be seen, of fat denominations.

"Here it is, your Excellency; a little ragged, but readable still."

The chancellor went over it carefully.

"Herr Captain, do you know this compatriot?"

"We fought side by side in the American war. I saw no irregularity in his papers. I am rather astonished to see him here and not at the police bureau, if any question has arisen over his passports."

"Fought side by side," the chancellor repeated thoughtfully. "Then he is no stranger to you?"

"I do not say that. We were, however, in the same cavalry, only in different troops. Grumbach, you have your honorable discharge with you?"

Grumbach went into his wallet still again. This document the chancellor read with an interest foreign to the affair under his hand. Presently he laughed softly. Why, he could not readily have told.

"I am sorry, Herr Grumbach. All this unnecessary trouble simply because of the word Bavaria."

"No trouble at all, your Excellency," restoring his papers. "I have seen the inside of a real palace, and I never expected such an honor."

"How long will you be making your visit?"

"Only a few days, your Excellency. Then I shall proceed to Bavaria."

"Your excellency has no further orders?" said the head gardener patiently.

"Good Heaven, Breunner, I had forgotten all about you! There is nothing more. Gentlemen, your pardon for having detained you so long. Herr Captain, you will return with me to the ball-room?"

"If your excellency will excuse me, no. I am tired. I shall return to the hotel with Herr Grumbach."

"As you please. Good night."

The three left the cabinet under various emotions. The sub-chief bowed himself off at the gates, and Carmichael and Grumbach crossed the Platz leisurely.

"How did you come by that Bavarian passport?" asked Carmichael abruptly.

"It is a forgery, my friend, but his excellency will never find that out."

"You have me all at sea. Why did he bring in the head gardener and leave him standing there all that while?"

"He had a sound purpose, but it fell. The head gardener did not recognize me."

"Do you know him?"

"Yes. He is my elder brother."

CHAPTER VIII

THE KING'S LETTER

The ambassador from Jugendheit, Baron von Steinbock, was not popular in Dreiberg, at least not among the people, who still held to the grand duke's idea that the kingdom had been behind the abduction of the Princess Hildegarde. The citizens scowled at his carriage, they scowled at the mention of his name, they scowled whenever they passed the embassy, which stood in the heart of the fashionable residences in the Koenig Strasse. Never a hot-headed Dreiberger passed the house without a desire to loot it, to scale the piked fence and batter in the doors and windows. Steinbock himself was a polished, amiable gentleman, in no wise meriting this ill-feeling. The embassy was in all manner the most important in Dreiberg, though Prussia and Austria overshadowed it in wealth and prestige.

At this moment the people gazed at the house less in rancor than in astonishment. The king of Jugendheit was to marry her serene highness! It was a bad business, a bad business; no good would come of it. The great duke was a weak man, after all.

The menials in and about the embassy felt the new importance of their positions. So then, imagine the indignation of the majordomo, when, summoned at dusk one evening to the carriage gates, three or four days after the portentous news had issued from the palace, he found only a ragged and grimy carter who demanded peremptorily to be admitted and taken to his excellency at once.

"Be off with you, ragamuffin!" growled the majordomo.

"Be quick; open the gates!" replied the carter, swinging his whip threateningly.

"Go away!" The majordomo spun on his heels contemptuously.

"I will skin you alive," vowed the carter, striking the iron with the butt of his whip, "if you do not open these gates immediately. Open!"

There was real menace this time. Could the fellow be crazy? The majordomo concluded to temporize.

"My good man," he said conciliatorily, "you have brains. You ought to know that his excellency will receive no man in your condition. If you do not stop hammering on those bars, I shall send for the police."

The carter thrust a hand through the grill. There was a ring on one of his fingers.

"Imbecile, set your eye on that and admit me without more ado!"

The majordomo was thunderstruck. Indeed, a blast from the heavens would have jarred him less.

"Open, then!"

The majordomo threw back the bolts and the carter pushed his way in. That ring on the carter's finger? The majordomo felt himself slipping into a fantastic dream.

"Take me to the baron."

Vastly subdued the majordomo preceded the carter into the office of the embassy. There he left the strange guest and went in search of the baron. The ambassador was in his study, reading.

"Your Excellency, there is a man in the office who desires to see you quickly."

The ambassador laid down his book. "Upon what pretense did he gain admittance at this hour?" he demanded.

"I refused him admittance, your Excellency, because he was dressed like a carter. - "

"A carter!" The ambassador wrathfully jumped to his feet.

"One moment, your Excellency. He wore a ring on his finger, and I could not refuse him."

"A ring, you say?"

Guarding his voice with his hand, the majordomo whispered two words.

"Here, and dressed like a carter? What the devil!" The ambassador rushed from the study.

It was dark in the embassy office. Quickly the ambassador lighted some candles. Gas would be too bright for such a meeting.

Harold MacGrath

"Well, your Excellency?" said a voice from the leather lounge.

"Who are you?" For this was not the voice the baron expected to hear.

"My name at present does not matter. The news I bring is far more important. His majesty emphatically declines any alliance with the House of Ehrenstein."

The ambassador stumbled into a chair, his mind dulled, his shoulders inert. This was a blow.

"Declines?" he murmured.

"He repudiates his uncle's negotiations absolutely."

"Damnation!" swore the ambassador, coming to life once more.

"The exact word used by the prince; in fact, the word has become common property in the last forty-eight hours. Now then, what's to be done? What do you suggest?"

"This means war. The duke will never swallow such an insult."

"War! It looks as if you and I, Baron, shall not accompany the king of Prussia into Alsace-Lorraine. We shall have entertainment at home."

"This is horrible!"

"The devil of a muddle!"

"But what possessed the prince to blunder like this?"

"The prince really is not to blame. Our king, Baron, is a young colt. A few months ago he gave his royal uncle carte blanche to seek a wife for him. Politics demanded an alliance between Jugendheit and Ehrenstein. There have been too many years of useless antagonism. On the head of this bolt from Heaven comes the declaration of his majesty that he will marry any other princess on the continent."

"They will pull this place down, brick by brick!"

"Let them! We have ten thousand more troops than Ehrenstein."

"You young men are a pack of fools!"

"Softly, Baron."

"You would like nothing better than war."

"Unless it is peace."

"Where is the king?"

The carter smiled. "He is hunting, they say, with the crown prince of Bavaria."

"But you, why have you come dressed like this?"

"That is a little secret which I am not at liberty to disclose."

"But, great God, what's to be done?"

"Lie," urbanely.

"What good will lies do?"

Harold MacGrath

"They will suspend the catastrophe till we are ready to meet it. The marriage is not to take place till spring. That will give us plenty of time. After the coronation his majesty may be brought to reason. This marriage must not fall through now. The grand duke will not care to become the laughing-stock of Europe. The prince's advice is for you to go about your affairs as usual. Only one man must be taken into your confidence, and that man is Herbeck. If any one can straighten out his end of the tangle it is he. He is a big man, of fertile invention; he will understand. If this thing falls through his honors will fall with it. He will work toward peace, though from what I have learned the duke would not shun war."

"Where is the prince?"

"Wherever he is, he is working for the best interests of the state. Don't worry about his royal highness; he's a man."

"When did you come?"

"This morning. Though I have been here before in this same guise."

"There is the Bavarian princess," remarked the ambassador musingly.

"Ha! A good thought! But the king is romantic; she is older than he, and ugly."

"You are not telling me everything," intuitively.

"I know it. I am telling you all that is at present necessary."

"You make me the unhappiest man in the kingdom! I have worked so hard and long toward this end. When did the king decline this alliance?"

"Evidently the moment he heard of it. I have his letter in my pocket. I am requested to read it to you. Listen:

"'MY ILLUSTRIOUS AND INDUSTRIOUS UNCLE: I regret exceedingly that at this late day I should cause you political embarrassment; but when I gave my consent to the espousal of any of the various princesses at liberty, surely it was understood that Ehrenstein was not to be considered. I refuse to marry the daughter of the man who privately strove to cover my father with contumely, who dared impute to him a crime that was any man's but my father's. I realize that certain policies called for this stroke on your part, but it can not be. My dear uncle, you have digged a fine pit, and I hope you will find a safe way out of it. I refuse to marry the Princess Hildegarde. This is final. It can be arranged without any discredit to the duke or to yourself. Let it be said that her serene highness has thrown me over. I shan't go to war about it.

"'FREDERICK.'"

"Observe 'My illustrious and industrious uncle'!" laughed the carter without mirth. "Our king, you will see, has a graceful style."

"Your tone is not respectful," warned the ambassador.

"Neither is the state of my mind. Oh, my king is a fine fellow; he will settle down like his father before him; but to-day - " The carter dropped his arms dejectedly.

"There is something going on."

"What, you are likely to learn at any moment. Pardon me,

Baron, but if I dared I would tell you all. But his highness' commands are over me and I must obey them. It would be a mental relief to tell some one."

"Curse these opera-dancers!"

The carter laughed. "Aye, where kings are concerned. But you do him injustice. Frederick is as mild as Strephon." He gained his feet. He was young, pleasant of face, but a thorough soldier.

"You are Lieutenant von Radenstein!" cried the ambassador. "I recognize you now."

"Thanks, your Excellency!"

"You are in the royal household, the regent's invisible arm. I have heard a good deal about you. I knew your father well."

"Again, thanks. Now, the regent has heard certain rumors regarding an American named Carmichael, a consul. He is often seen with her highness. Rather an extraordinary privilege."

"Rest your mind there, Lieutenant. This Carmichael is harmless. You understand, her highness has not always been surrounded by royal etiquette. She has had her freedom too long not to grow restive under restraint. The American is a pleasant fellow, but not worth considering. Americans will never understand the ways of court life. Still, he is a gentleman, and so far there is nothing compromising in that situation. He can be eliminated at any time."

"This is reassuring. You will see the chancellor to-night and show him this letter?"

"I will, and God help us all to straighten out this blunder!"

"Amen to that! One word more, and then I'm off. If a butcher or a baker, or even a mountaineer pulls the bell-cord and shows this ring, admit him without fail. He will have vital news. And now, good night and good luck to your excellency."

For half an hour the ambassador remained staring at the candlesticks. By and by he resumed his chair. What should he do? Where should he begin? Suppose the chancellor should look at the situation adversely, from the duke's angle of vision, should the duke learn? There was but one thing to do and that was to go boldly to Herbeck and lay the matter before him frankly. Neither Jugendheit nor Ehrenstein wanted war. The chancellor was wise; it would be better to dally with the truth than needlessly to sacrifice ten thousand lives. But what had the lieutenant further to conceal? The ambassador wanted no dinner. He rang for his hat and coat, and twenty minutes later he was in the chancellor's cabinet.

"You seem out of health, Baron," was the chancellor's greeting.

"I am indeed that, Count. I received a letter to-day from the prince regent. It was sent to him by his majesty, who is hunting in Bavaria. Read it, Count, but I pray to you to do nothing hastily."

The chancellor did not open the letter, he merely balanced it. That so light a thing should be so heavy with dark portents! His accustomed pallor assumed a grayish tinge.

"So his majesty declines?" he said evenly.

"You have already heard?" cried the amazed ambassador.

"Nothing; I surmise. The hour, your appearance, the letter - to what else could they point? I was afraid all along. Strange instinct we have at times. The regent is to be pitied; he took too much for granted. He has been used to power one day too long. Ah, if his majesty could but see her, could only know how lovely she is in heart and mind and face! Is she not worthy a crown?"

"Herbeck, nothing would please me better, nothing would afford my country greater pleasure and satisfaction, than to see this marriage consummated. It would nail that baseless lie which has so long been current."

"I believe you. We two peoples should be friendly. It has taken me months to bring this matter round. The duke rebelled; her highness scorned the hand of Frederick. One by one I had to overcome their objections - to this end. The past refuses to be buried. Still, if you saw all the evidence in the case you would not blame the duke for his attitude."

"But those documents are rank forgeries!"

"So they may be, but that has not been proved."

"Why should his late majesty abduct the daughter of the grand duke? For what benefits? To what end? Ah, Count, if some motive could be brought forward, some motive that could stand!"

"Motives, my friend? They spring from the most unheard-of places. And motives in action are always based on impulses. But let us waste no time on retrospection. It is the present which confronts us. You do not want war."

"No more do you."

"What remedy do you suggest?"

"I ask, nay, I plead that question of you."

"I represent the offended party." The chancellor's gaunt features lighted with a transient smile. "Proceed, Baron."

"I suggest, then, that the duke must not know."

"Agreed. Go on."

"You will put the matter before her highness."

"That will be difficult."

"Let her repudiate the negotiations. Let her say that she has changed her mind. His majesty is quite willing that the humiliation be his."

"That is generous. But suppose she has set her heart on the crown of Jugendheit? What then?"

The baron bit the ends of his mustache.

"Suppose that?" the chancellor pressed relentlessly.

"In that event, the affair is no longer in our hands but in God's."

"As all affairs are. Is there no way of changing the king's mind?"

"Read the letter, Count," said the ambassador.

Herbeck hunted for the postmark: Bavaria. He read the letter. There was nothing between the lines. It was the work of rather an irresponsible boy.

"May I take this to her highness?" asked the chancellor.

"I'm afraid - "

"I promise its contents will not go beyond her eye."

"I will take the risk."

"His majesty is very young," was the chancellor's comment.

"Young! He is a child. He has been in his palace twice in ten years. He is travel-mad. He has been wandering in France, Holland, England, Belgium. He tells his uncle to play the king till the coronation. Imagine it! And the prince has found this authority so pleasant and natural that he took it for granted that his majesty would marry whomever he selected for him. To have allowed us to go forward, as we have done, believing that he had the whole confidence of the king!"

Herbeck consulted his watch. It was half after six. Her highness did not dine till eight.

"I shall go to her highness immediately, Baron. I shall return the letter by messenger, and he will tell you the result of the interview."

"God be with you," said the ambassador, preparing to take his leave, "for all women are contrary."

After the baron was gone the chancellor paced the room with halting step. Then, toward the wraith of his ambition he waved a hand as if to explain how futile are the schemes of men. He shook himself free from this idle moment and proceeded to the apartments of her highness. Would she toss aside this crown, or would she fight for it? He found her alone.

"Well, my good fairy, what is in your magic wand to-night?" she asked. How fond she was of this great good man, and how lonely he always seemed!

He saluted her hand respectfully. "I am not a good fairy to-night, your Highness. On the contrary, I am an ogre. I have here a letter. I have given my word that its contents shall not be repeated to the duke, your father. If I let you read it, will you agree to that?"

"And who has written this letter?" non-committally.

"His majesty, the king of Jugendheit," slowly.

"A letter from the king?" she cried, curious. "Should it not be brought to me on a golden salver?"

"It is probable that I am bringing it to you at the end - of a bayonet," solemnly. "If the duke learns its contents the inevitable result will be war."

A silence fell upon them and grew. This was the bitterest moment but one in the chancellor's life.

"I believe," she said finally, "that it will not be necessary to read his majesty's letter. He declines the honor of my hand: is that not it?"

The chancellor signified that it was.

"Ah!" with a note of pride in her voice and a flash in her eyes. "And I?"

"You will tell the duke that you have changed your mind," gravely.

"Do princesses change their minds like this?"

"They have often done so."

"In spite of publicity?"

"Yes, your Highness."

"And if I refuse to change my mind?"

"I am resigned to any and all events."

"War." Her face was serious. "And what has the king to suggest?"

"He proposes to accept the humiliation of being rejected by you."

"Why, this is a gallant king! Pouff! There goes a crown of thistledown." She smiled at the chancellor, then she laughed. There was nothing but youth in the laughter, youth and gladness. "Oh, I knew that you were a good fairy. Listen to me. I declare to you that I am happier at this moment than I have been in days. To marry a man I have never seen, to become the wife of a man who is nothing to me, whose looks, character, and habits are unknown; why, I have lived in a kind of horror. You did not find me soon enough; there are yet some popular ideas in my head which are alien to the minds of princesses. I am free!" And she uttered the words as with the breath of spring.

The chancellor's shoulders drooped a trifle more, and his hand closed down over the letter. Otherwise there was no notable change in his appearance. He was always guarding the muscles of his face. Inscrutability is the first lesson of the diplomat; and he had learned it thirty years before.

"There will be no war," resumed her highness. "I know my father; our wills may clash, but in this instance mine shall be the stronger."

"But this is not the end."

"You mean that there will be other kings?" She had not thought of this, and some of the brightness vanished from her face.

"Yes, there will be other kings. I am sorry. What young girl has not her dream of romance? But princesses must not have romances. Yours, my child, must be a political marriage. It is a harsh decree."

"Have not princesses married commoners?"

"Never wisely. Your highness will not make a mistake like that."

"My highness will or will not marry, as she pleases. Am I a chattel, that I am to be offered across this frontier or that?"

The chancellor moved uneasily. "If your highness loved out of your class, which I know you do not, I should be worried."

"And if I did?" with a rebel tilt to her chin.

"Till that moment arrives I shall not borrow trouble. You will, then, tell the duke that you have changed your mind, that you have reconsidered?"

"This evening. Now, godfather, you may kiss her serene highness on the forehead."

"This honor to me?" The chancellor trembled.

"Even so."

He did not touch her with Ne hands, but the kiss he put on her forehead was a benediction.

"You may go now," she said, "for I shall need the whole room to dance in. I am free, if only for a little while!"

Outside the door the chancellor paused. She was singing. It was the same aria he had heard that memorable night when he found her in the dim garret.

CHAPTER IX

GRETCHEN'S DAY

Gretchen was always up when the morning was rosy, when the trees were still dark and motionless, and the beads of dew white and frostlike. For what is better than to meet the day as it comes over the mountains, and silence breaks here and there, in the houses and streets, in the fields and the vineyards? Let old age, which has played its part and taken to the wings of the stage, let old age loiter in the morning, but not green years. Gretchen awoke as the birds awoke, with snatches and little trills of song. To her nearest neighbors there was about her that which reminded them of the regularity of a good clock; when they heard her voice they knew it was time to get up.

She was always busy in the morning. The tinkle of the bell outside brought her to the door, and her two goats came pattering in to be relieved of their creamy burden. Gretchen was fond of them; they needed no care at all. The moment she had milked them they went tinkling off to the steep pastures.

Even in midsummer the dawn was chill in Dreiberg. She blew on her fingers. The fire was down to the last ember; so she went into the cluttered courtyard and broke into pieces one of the limbs she had carried up from the valley earlier in the season. The fire renewed its cheerful crackle, the kettle boiled briskly, and the frugal breakfast was under way.

There was daily one cup of coffee, but neither Gretchen nor her grandmother claimed this luxury; it was for the sick woman on the third floor. Sometimes at the Black Eagle she had a cup when her work was done, but to Gretchen the aroma excelled the taste. Her grandmother's breakfast and her own out of the way, she carried the coffee and bread and a hot brick up to the invalid. The woman gave her two crowns a week to serve this morning meal. Gretchen would have cheerfully done the work for nothing.

What the character of the woman's illness was Gretchen hadn't an idea, but there could be no doubt that she was ill, desperately, had the goose-girl but known it. Her face was thin and the bones were visible under the drum-like skin; her hands were merely claws. But she would have no doctor; she would have no care save that which Gretchen gave her. Sometimes she remained in bed all the day. She had been out of the house but once since she came. She mystified the girl, for she never complained, never asked questions, talked but little, and always smiled kindly when the pillow was freshened.

"Good morning, Fraeu," said Gretchen.

"Good morning, *Liebchen*."

"I have brought you a brick this morning, for it will be cold till the sun is high."

"Thank you."

Gretchen pulled the deal table to the side of the cot, poured out the coffee, and buttered the bread.

"I ought not to drink coffee, but it is the only thing that warms me. You have been very patient with me."

"I am glad to help you."

"And that is why I love you. Now, I have some instructions to give you this morning. Presently I shall be leaving, and there will be something besides crowns."

"You are thinking of leaving?"

"Yes. When I go I shall not come back. Under my pillow there is an envelope. You will find it and keep it."

Gretchen, young and healthy, touched not this melancholy undercurrent. She accepted the words at their surface value. She knew nothing about death except by hearsay.

"You will promise to take it?"

"Yes, Fraeu."

"Thanks, little gosling. I have an errand for you this morning. It will take you to the palace."

"To the palace?" echoed Gretchen.

"Yes. Does that frighten you?"

"No, Fraeu; it only surprises me. What shall I do?"

"You will seek her highness and give her this note."

"The princess?" Gretchen sadly viewed her wooden shoes

and roughened hands.

"Never mind your hands and feet; your face will open any gate or door for you."

"I have never been to the palace. Will they not laugh and turn me out?"

"If they try that, demand to see his excellency, Count von Herbeck, and say that you came from forty Krumerweg."

Gretchen shuddered with a mixture of apprehension and delight. To meet and speak to all these great ones!

"And if I can not get in?"

"You will have no trouble. Be sure, though, to give the note to no one but her highness. There will be no answer. All I ask is that when you return you will tell me if you were successful. You may go."

Gretchen put the note away and went down-stairs. She decked her beautiful head with a little white cap, which she wore only on Sundays and at the opera, and braided and beribboned her hair. It never occurred to her that there was anything unusual in the incident. It was only when she came out into the Koenig Strasse that the puzzle of it came to her forcibly. Who was this old woman who thought nothing of writing a letter to her serene highness? And who were her nocturnal visitors? Gretchen had no patience with puzzles, so she let her mind revel in the thought that she was to see and speak to the princess whom she admired and revered. What luck! How smoothly the world was beginning to run!

Being of a discerning mind, she idled about the Platz till after nine, for it had been told to her that the great sleep rather late in the morning. What should she say to her serene highness? What kind of a curtsy should she make? These and a hundred other questions flitted through her head. At least she would wear no humble, servile air. For Gretchen was a bit of a socialist. Did not Herr Goldberg, whom the police detested, did he not say that all men were equal? And surely this sweeping statement included women! She attended secret meetings in the damp cellar of the Black Eagle, and, while she laughed at some of the articles in the propaganda, she received seriously enough that which proclaimed her the equal of any one. So long as she obeyed nature's laws and Heaven's, was she not indeed the equal of queens and princesses, who, it was said, did not always obey these laws?

With a confidence born of right and innocence, she proceeded toward the east or side gates of the palace. The sentry smiled at her.

"I have a letter for her serene highness," she said.

"Leave it."

"I am under orders to give it to her highness herself."

"Good day, then!" laughed the soldier. "You can not enter the gardens without a permit."

Gretchen remembered. "Will you send some one to his excellency the chancellor and tell him I have come from number forty Krumerweg?"

"Krumerweg? The very name ought to close any gate. But, girl, are you speaking truthfully?"

Gretchen exhibited the note. He scratched his chin, perplexed.

"Run along. If they ask me, I'll say that I didn't see you." The sentry resumed his beat.

Gretchen stepped inside the gates, and the real beauty of the gardens was revealed to her for the first time. Strange flowers she had never seen before, plants with great broad leaves, grass-like carpet, and giant ferns, unlike anything she had plucked in the valleys and the mountains. It was all a fairy-land. There were marble urns with hanging vines, and marble statues. She loitered in this pebbled path and that, forgetful of her errand. Even had her mind been filled with the importance of it, she did not know where to go to find the proper entrance.

A hand grasped her rudely by the arm.

"What are you doing here?" thundered the head gardener. "Be off with you! Don't you know that no one is allowed in here without a permit?"

Gretchen wrenched free her arm. She was angry.

"How dare you touch me like that?"

Something in her glance, which was singularly arrogant, cooled even the warm-blooded Hermann.

"But you live in Dreiberg and ought to know."

"You could have told me without bruising my arm," defiantly.

"I am sorry if I hurt you, but you ought to have known better. By which sentry did you pass?" for there was that about her beauty which made him suspicious regarding the sentry's imperviousness to it.

"Hermann!"

Gretchen and the head gardener whirled. Through a hedge which divided the formal gardens from the tennis and archery grounds came a young woman in riding-habit. She carried a book in one hand and a riding-whip in the other.

"What is the trouble, Hermann?" she inquired. "Your voice was something high."

"Your Highness, this young woman here had the impudence to walk into the gardens and stroll about as nice as you please," indignantly.

"Has she stolen any flowers or trod on any of the beds?"

"Why, no, your Highness; but - "

"What is the harm, then?"

"But it is not customary, your Highness. If we permitted this on the part of the people, the gardens would be ruined in a week."

"We, you and I, Hermann," said her highness, with a smile that won Gretchen on the spot, "we will overlook this first offense. Perhaps this young lady had some errand and lost her way."

"Yes, Highness," replied Gretchen eagerly.

"Ah! You may go, Hermann."

"Your highness alone with - "

"Go at once," kindly, but with royal firmness.

Hermann bowed, gathered up his pruning knives and scissors which he had let fall, and stalked down the path. What was it? he wondered. She was a princess in all things save her lack of coldness toward the people. It was wrong to meet them in this way, it was not in order. Her highness had lived too long among them. She would never rid herself of the idea that the humble had hearts and minds like the exalted.

As the figure of the head gardener diminished and shortly vanished behind a bed of palms, her highness laughed brightly, and Gretchen, to her own surprise, found herself laughing also, easily and without constraint.

"Whom were you seeking?" her highness asked, rather startled by the undeniable beauty of this peasant.

"I was seeking your serene highness. I live at number forty the Krumerweg, and the sick woman gave me this note for you."

"Krumerweg?" Her highness reached for the note and read it, and as she read tears gathered in her eyes. "Follow me," she said. She led Gretchen to a marble bench and sat down. Gretchen remained on her feet respectfully. "What is your name?"

"Gretchen, Highness."

"Well, Gretchen, sit down."

"In your presence, Highness?" aghast.

"Don't bother about my presence on a morning like this. Sit down."

This was a command and Gretchen obeyed with alacrity. It

would not be difficult, thought Gretchen, to love a princess like this, who was not only lovely but sensible. The two sat mutely. They were strangely alike. Their eyes nearly matched, their hair, even the shape of their faces. They were similarly molded, too; only, one was slender and graceful, after the manner of fashion, while the other was slender and graceful directly from the hands of nature. The health of outdoors was visible in their fine skins and clear eyes. The marked difference lay, of course, in their hands. The princess had never toiled with her fingers except on the piano. Gretchen had plucked geese and dug vegetables with hers. They were rough, but toil had not robbed them of their natural grace.

"How was she?" her highness asked.

"About the same, Highness."

"Have you wondered why she should write to me?"

"Highness, it was natural that I should," was Gretchen's frank admission.

"She took me in when nobody knew who I was, clothed and fed me, and taught me music so that some day I should not be helpless when the battle of life began. Ah," impulsively, "had I my way she would be housed in the palace, not in the lonely Krumerweg. But my father does not know that she is in Dreiberg; and we dare not tell him, for he still believes that she had something to do with my abduction." Then she stopped. She was strangely making this peasant her confidante. What a whim!

"Highness, that could not be."

"No, Gretchen; she had nothing to do with it." Her highness

leveled her gaze at the flowers, but her eyes saw only the garret or the barnlike loneliness of the opera during rehearsals.

Gretchen did not move. She saw that her highness was dreaming; and she herself had dreams.

"Do you like music?"

"Highness, I am always singing."

"La-la-la!" sang the princess capriciously.

"La-la-la!" sang Gretchen smiling. Her voice was not purer or sweeter; it was merely stronger, having been accustomed to the open air.

"Brava!" cried the princess, dropping book and whip and folding the note inside the book. "Who taught you to sing?"

"Nobody, highness."

"What do you do?"

"I am a goose-girl; in the fall and winter I work at odd times in the Black Eagle."

"The Black Eagle? A tavern?"

"Yes, Highness."

"Tell me all about yourself."

This was easy for Gretchen; there was so little.

"Neither mother nor father. Our lives are something alike. A handsome girl like you must have a sweetheart."

Gretchen blushed. "Yes, Highness. I am to be married soon. He is a vintner. I would not trade him for your king, Highness," with a spice of boldness.

Her highness did not take offense; rather she liked this frankness. In truth, she liked any one who spoke to her on equal footing; it was a taste of the old days when she herself could have chosen a vintner and married him, with none to say her nay. Now she was only a pretty bird in a gilded cage. She could fly, but whenever she did so she blundered painfully against the bright wires. If there was any envy between these two, it existed in the heart of the princess only. To be free like this, to come and go at will, to love where the heart spoke! She surrendered to another vagrant impulse.

"Gretchen, I do not think I shall marry the king of Jugendheit."

Gretchen grew red with pride. Her highness was telling her state secrets!

"You love some one else, Highness?" How should a goose-girl know that such a question was indelicate?

Her highness did not blush; the color in her cheeks receded. She fondled the heart-shaped locket which she invariably wore round her throat. That this peasant girl should thus boldly put a question she herself had never dared to press!

"You must not ask questions like that, Gretchen."

"Pardon, Highness; I did not think." Gretchen was disturbed.

But the princess comforted her with: "I know it. There are some questions which should not be asked even by the heart."

This was not understandable to Gretchen; but the locket pleased her eye. Her highness, observing her interest, slipped the trinket from her neck and laid it in Gretchen's hand.

"Open it," she said. "It is a picture of my mother, whom I do not recollect having ever seen. Wait," as Gretchen turned it about helplessly.

"I will open it for you." Click!

Gretchen sighed deeply. To have had a mother so fair and pretty! She hadn't an idea how her own mother had looked; indeed, being sensible and not given much to conjuring, she had rarely bothered her head about it. Still, as she gazed at this portrait, the sense of her isolation and loneliness drew down upon her, and she in her turn sought the flowers and saw them not. After a while she closed the locket and returned it.

"So you love music?" picking up the safer thread.

"Ah, yes, Highness."

"Do you ever go to the opera?"

"As often as I can afford. I am very poor."

"I will give you a ticket for the season. How can I reward you for bringing this message? Don't have any false pride. Ask for something."

"Well, then, Highness, give me an order on the grand duke's

head vintner for a place."

"For the man who is to become your husband?"

"Yes, Highness."

"You shall have it to-morrow. Now, come with me. I am going to take you to Herr Ernst. He is the director of the opera. He rehearses in the court theater this morning."

Gretchen, undetermined whether she was waking or dreaming, followed the princess. She was serenely unafraid, to her own great wonder. Who could describe her sensations as she passed through marble halls, up marble staircases, over great rugs so soft that her step faltered? Her wooden shoes made a clatter whenever they left the rugs, but she stepped as lightly as she could. She heard music and voices presently, and the former she recognized. As her highness entered the Bijou Theater, the Herr Direktor stopped the music. In the little gallery, which served as the royal box, sat several ladies and gentlemen of the court, the grand duke being among them. Her highness nodded at them brightly.

"Good morning, Herr Direktor."

"Good morning, your Highness."

"I have brought you a prima donna," touching Gretchen with her whip.

The Herr Direktor showed his teeth; her highness was always playing some jest.

"What shall she sing in, your Highness? We are rehearsing *The Bohemian Girl*."

The chorus and singers on the little stage exchanged smiles.

"I want your first violin," said her highness.

"Anton!"

A youth stood up in the orchestral pit.

"Now, your Highness?" said the Herr Direktor.

"Try her voice."

And the Herr Direktor saw that she was not smiling. He bade the violinist to draw his bow over a single note.

"Imitate it, Gretchen," commanded her highness; "and don't be afraid of the Herr Direktor or of the ladies and gentlemen in the gallery."

Gretchen lifted her voice. It was sweeter and mellower than the violin.

"Again!" the Herr Direktor cried, no longer curious.

Without apparent effort Gretchen passed from one note to another, now high, now low, or strong or soft; a trill, a run. The violinist, of his own accord, began the jewel song from *Faust*. Gretchen did not know the words, but she carried the melody without mishap. And then, *I Dreamt I Dwelt in Marble Halls*. This song she knew word for word, and ah, she sang it with strange and haunting tenderness! One by one the musicians dropped their instruments to their knees. The grand duke in the gallery leaned over the velvet-buffered railing. All realized that a great voice was being tried before them. The Herr Direktor struck his music-stand sharply. It was enough.

"Your highness has played a fine jest this day. Where does madame your guest sing, in Berlin or Vienna?"

"In neither," answered her highness, mightily gratified with Gretchen's success. "She lives in Dreiberg, and till this morning I doubt if I ever saw her before."

The Herr Direktor stared blankly from her highness to Gretchen, and back to her highness again. Then he grasped it. Here was one of those moments when the gods make gifts to mortals.

"Can you read music?" he asked.

"No, Herr," said Gretchen.

"That is bad. You have a great voice, Fraeulein. Well, I shall teach you. I shall make you a great singer. It is hard work."

"I have always worked hard."

"Good! Your Highness, a thousand thanks! What is your name?" to Gretchen. She told him. "It is a good name. Come to me Monday at the opera and I shall put you into good hands. Some day you will be rich, and I shall become great because I found you."

Then, with the artist's positive indifference to the presence of exalted blood, he turned his back upon the two young women and roused his men from the trance.

"So, Gretchen," said her highness, when the two came out again into the garden, "you are to be rich and famous. That will be fine."

"Thanks, Highness, thanks! God grant the day to come when

I may be of service to you!" Gretchen kissed the hands of her benefactress.

"Whenever you wish to see the gardens," added the princess, "the gates will be open for you."

As Gretchen went back to the Krumerweg her wooden shoes were golden slippers and her rough homespun, silk. Rich! Famous! She saw the opera ablaze with lights, she heard the roll of applause. She saw the horn of plenty pouring its largess from the fair sky. Rainbow dreams! But Gretchen never became a prima donna. There was something different on the knees of the gods.

CHAPTER X

AFFAIRS OF STATE

The grand duke stamped back and forth with a rumble as of distant thunder. He would search the very deeps of this matter. He was of a patient mold, but this was the final straw. He would have his revenge if it upset the whole continent. They would play with him, eh? Well, they had loosed the lion this time. He had sent his valet to summon her highness and Herbeck.

"And tell them to put everything else aside."

He kneaded the note in his hand powerfully. It was anonymous, but it spoke clearly like truth. It had been left with one of the sentries, who declared that a small boy had delivered it. The sender remained undiscoverable.

His highness had just that hour returned from the military field. He was tired; and it was not the psychological moment for a thing like this to turn up. Had he not opposed it for months? And now, having surrendered against his better judgment, this gratuitous affront was offered him! It was damnable. He smote the offending note. He would soon find out whether it was true or not. Then he flung the thing violently to the floor. But he realized that this burst of fury would not translate the muddle, so he stooped and recovered the missive. He laughed, but the laughter had a grim Homeric sound. War! Nothing less. He was prepared for it. Twenty thousand troops were now in the valley, and there were twenty thousand reserves. What Franz Josef of Austria or William of Prussia said did not amount to the snap of his two fingers. To avenge himself of the wrongs so long endured of Jugendheit, to wipe out the score with blood! Did they think that he was in his dotage, to offer an insult of this magnitude? They should see, aye, that they should! It did not matter that the news reached him through subterranean channels or by treachery; there was truth here, and that sufficed.

"Enter!" he cried, as some one knocked on the door.

Herbeck came in, as calm, as imperturbable as ever.

"Your highness sent for me?"

"I did. Why the devil couldn't you have left well enough alone? Read this!" flinging the note down on his desk.

Herbeck picked it up and worked out the creases. When he had read to the final word, his hand, even as the duke's, closed spasmodically over the stiff paper.

"Well?" The query tingled with rage.

The answer on the chancellor's lips was not uttered. Hildegarde came in. She blew a kiss at her father, who caught the hand and drew her toward him. He embraced her and kissed her brow.

"What is it, father?"

Herbeck waited.

"Read," said the duke.

As the last word left Herbeck's lips, she slipped from her father's arms and looked with pity at the chancellor.

"What do you think of this, Hildegarde?"

"Why, father, I think it is the very best thing in the world," dryly.

"An insult like this?" The duke grew rigid. "You accept it calmly, in this fashion?"

"Shall I weep and tear my hair over a boy I have never seen? No, thank you. I was about to make known to you this very evening that I had reconsidered the offer. I shall never marry his majesty."

"A fine time!" The duke's hand trembled. "Why, in God's name, did you not refuse when the overtures were first made? The truth, Herbeck, the whole truth; for there is something more than this."

Herbeck, in few words and without evasion, explained the situation.

"Your Highness, the regent is really not to blame, for his majesty had given him free rein in the matter; and his royal highness, working as I have been for the best interests of the two countries, never dreamed that the king would rebel. All my heart and all my mind have been working toward this end, toward a greater peace and prosperity. The king has been generous enough to leave the publicity in our hands; that is to say, he agrees to accept the humiliation of being rejected by her serene highness."

"That is very generous of him!" said the duke sarcastically. "Send for Ducwitz."

"Ducwitz, your Highness?" cried the chancellor, chilled.

"Immediately!"

"Father!"

"Must I give an order twice?"

"Your Highness, if you call Ducwitz I shall surrender my portfolio to you." The chancellor spoke without anger, quietly but firmly.

"Do so. There are others to take up your work." The duke, for the moment, had thrown reason to the winds. Revenge, the clamor of revenge, was all the voice he heard.

The chancellor bowed, turned to leave the room, when Hildegarde flew to the duke's side and snatched at his sleeve.

"Father, you are mad!"

"At least I am master in Ehrenstein. Herbeck, you will have the kindness to summon General Ducwitz."

"Your Highness," replied Herbeck, "I have worked long and faithfully in your service. I can not recollect that I ever asked one personal favor. But I do so now. Do not send for Ducwitz to-night. See him in the morning. This is no time for haste. You will throw the army into Jugendheit, and there will follow a bloody war. For I have to inform you that the prince regent, recognizing the false position he is in, has taken the ram by the horns. His troops are already bivouacked on the other side of the pass. This I learned to-day. He will not strike first; he will wait for you."

"I will have my revenge!" stubbornly.

"Father, listen to me. *I* am the affronted person; *I*, I alone, have the right to say what shall be done in the matter. And I say to you if you do these cruel things, dismiss his excellency and bring war and death to Ehrenstein, I will never forgive you, never, never! You are wrong, wrong, and I, your daughter, tell you so frankly. Leave it to me. There will be neither war nor humiliation."

As the duke gazed at her the wrath gathering in his throat receded and his admiration grew. His daughter! She was a princess, indeed, as she stood there, fearless, resolute, beautiful. And her very beauty gave recurrence to his wrath. A fool of a king he was, a fool of a king!

"My dear child," he said, "I have suffered too much at the hands of Jugendheit. It was my daughter the first time; it is my honor now," proudly.

"Will it balance war and devastation?" the girl asked quietly. "Is it not pride rather than honor? The prince regent made a pardonable blunder. Do not you, my father, make an unpardonable one. The king is without blame, for you appeal to his imagination as a man who deeply wronged his father. I harbor no ill-feeling against him or his uncle, because I look at the matter from an impersonal point of view; it was for the good of the state. This blunder can be undone; therefore it is not wise to double it, to make it irreparable."

"A Portia to the judgment!" said the chancellor, his eye kindling. "Let it all rest upon my shoulders. I alone am to blame. It was I who first suggested the alliance. We all have dreams, active or passive, futile or purposeful. My ambition was to bring about a real and lasting peace. Your Highness, I have failed signally. There is nothing to do now but to appoint my successor." All the chancellor's force and immobility of countenance gave way, and he looked the broken man.

Notwithstanding that he was generally hasty, the duke was a just man. In his heart of hearts he understood. He offered his hand, with half a smile; and when he smiled he was a handsome old man.

"You are bidding me farewell, your Highness?" said Herbeck.

"No, Count. I would not let you go for half my duchy. What should I do without your solid common sense? No; remain; we are both of us too old to quarrel. Even a duke may be a fool sometimes."

Herbeck laid his cold hand upon the duke's. Then he went over to her highness and kissed her hand gratefully, for it was truly at her feet the wreath of victory lay.

"Highness," he said softly, "you are the fairest, finest princess in the world, and you shall marry when you will."

"And where?"

"I would that I could make it so. But there is a penalty for being placed so high. We can not change this unwritten law."

"Heaven did not write it," she replied.

"No, my daughter," said the duke. "Man is at the bottom of

all the kinks and twists in this short life; not Heaven. But Herbeck is right; you shall marry *when* you will."

She sprang into his arms and kissed him. It was, however, a traitorous kiss; for she was saying in her heart that now she would never marry. Herbeck's eyes wandered to the portrait over the fireplace. It was the girl's mother.

The knock of the valet was again heard.

"Your Highness, there is a young woman, a peasant, who desires to speak to her serene highness."

"Where is she?" asked the duke.

"She is outside, your Highness."

"What! She enters the palace without any more trouble than this?"

"By my orders, father," said Hildegarde, who gathered that this privileged visitor must be Gretchen of the Krumerweg. "Admit her."

"Truly we are becoming socialists," said the duke, appealing to Herbeck, who replied with his usual grim smile.

Gretchen was ushered in. Her throat was a little full as she recognized the three most important persons in the grand duchy. Outwardly she was composed. She made a curtsy to which the duke replied with his most formal bow of state. The sparkle of amusement was in his eyes.

"The little goose-girl!" he said half-audibly.

"Yes, Highness." Gretchen's face was serious and her eyes

were mournful. She carried an envelope in her hand tightly.

"Come to me, Gretchen," said the princess.

"What is it?"

Gretchen's eyes roamed undecidedly from the duke to Herbeck.

"She is dead, Highness, and I found this letter under her pillow."

It was Herbeck's hand that took the envelope. But he did not open it at once.

"Dead?" Hildegarde's eyes filled.

"Who is dead?" demanded the duke.

"Emma Schultz, father. Oh, I know you will forgive me for this deception. She has been in Dreiberg for a month, dying, and I have often stolen out to see her." She let her tears fall unrestrained.

The duke stared at the rug. Presently he said: "Let her be buried in consecrated ground. Wrong or right, that chapter is closed, my child, and I am glad you made her last moments happy. It was like you. It was like your mother. What is in the letter, Herbeck?"

Herbeck was a strong man; he was always far removed from tears; but there was a mist over the usual clarity of his vision. He ripped down the flap. It was only a simple note to her serene highness, begging her to give the enclosed banknotes to one Gretchen who lived in the Krumerweg. The notes represented a thousand crowns.

"Take them, little goose-girl," said the duke; "your ship has come in. This will be your dowry."

An icy shiver ran up and down Gretchen's spine, a shiver of wonder, delight, terror. A thousand crowns! A fortune!

"Hold out your hand," requested Herbeck. One by one he laid the notes on the goose-girl's hand. "This is only a just reward for being kind and gentle to the unfortunate."

"And I shall add to it another thousand," said Hildegarde. "Give them to me, father."

In all, this fortune amounted to little more than four hundred dollars; but to Gretchen, frugal and thrifty, to whom a single crown was a large sum, to her it represented wealth. She was now the richest girl in the lower town. Dreams of kaleidoscopic variety flew through her head. Little there was, however, of jewels and gowns. This vast sum would be the buffer between her and hunger while she pursued the one great ambition of her life - music. She tried to speak, to thank them, but her voice was gone. Tears sprang into her eyes. She had the power to do no more than weep.

The duke was the first to relieve the awkwardness of the moment.

"Count, has it not occurred to you that we stand in the presence of two very beautiful young women?"

Herbeck scrutinized Gretchen with care; then he compared her with the princess. The duke was right. The goose-girl was not a whit the inferior of the princess. And the thing which struck him with most force was that, while each possessed a beauty individual to herself, it was not opposite, but strangely alike.

The goose-girl had returned to her gloomy Krumerweg, the princess had gone to her apartments, and Herbeck to his cabinet. The duke was alone. For a long period he stood before the portrait of his wife. The beauties of his courtship trooped past him; for God had given to the grand duke of Ehrenstein that which He denies most of us, high or low, a perfect love.

"Always, always, dear heart," he whispered; "in this life and in the life to come. To love, what is the sickle of death?"

He passed on to his secretary and opened a drawer. He laid a small bundle on the desk and untied the string. One by one he ranged the articles; two little yellow shoes, a little cloak trimmed with ermine. There had been a locket, but that was now worn by her highness.

CHAPTER XI

THE SOCIALISTS

Hermann Breunner lived in the granite lodge, just within the eastern gates of the royal gardens. He was a widower and shared the ample lodge with the undergardeners and their families. He lived with them, but signally apart. They gave him as much respect as if he had been the duke himself. He was a lonely, taciturn man, deeply concerned with his work, and a botanical student of no mean order. No comrade helped him pass away an evening in the chimney-corner, pipe in hand and good cheer in the mug. This isolation was not accidental, it was Hermann's own selection. He was a man of brooding moods, and there was no laughter in his withered heart, though the false sound of it crossed his lips at infrequent intervals.

He adjusted his heavy spectacles and held the note slantingly toward the candle. A note or a letter was a singular event in Hermann's life. Not that he looked forward with eagerness to receive them, but that there was no one existing who cared enough about him to write. This note left by the porter of the Grand Hotel moved him with surprise. It requested that he present himself at eight o'clock at the office of the hotel and ask to be directed to the room of Hans Grumbach.

Harold MacGrath

"Now, who is Hans Grumbach? I never knew or heard of a man of that name."

Nevertheless, he decided to go. Certainly this man Grumbach did not urge him without some definite purpose. He laid down his pipe, reached for his hat and coat - for in the lodge he generally went about in his shirt-sleeves - and went over to the hotel. The concierge, who knew Hermann, conducted him to room ten on the entresole. Hermann knocked. A voice bade him enter. Ah, it was the German-American, whose papers had puzzled his excellency.

"You wished to see me, Herr Grumbach?"

"Yes," said Grumbach, offering a chair.

Hermann accepted the courtesy with dignity. His host drew up another chair to the opposite side of the reading-table. The light overhead put both faces in a semishadow.

"You are Hermann Breunner," began Grumbach.

"Yes."

"You once had a brother named Hans."

Hermann grew rigid in his chair. "I have no brother," he replied, his voice dull and empty.

"Perhaps not now," continued Grumbach, "but you did have."

Hermann's head drooped. "My God, yes, I did have a brother; but he was a scoundrel."

Grumbach lighted a cigar. He did not offer one to Hermann,

who would have refused it.

"Perhaps he was a scoundrel. He is - dead!" softly.

"God's will be done!" But Hermann's face turned lighter.

"As a boy he loved you."

"And did I not love him?" said Hermann fiercely. "Did I not worship that boy, who was to me more like a son than a brother? Had not all the brothers and sisters died but he? But you - who are you to recall these things?"

"I knew your brother; I knew him well. He was not a scoundrel; only weak. He went to America and became successful in business. He fought with the North in the war. He was not a coward; he did his fighting bravely and honorably."

"Oh, no; Hans could never, have been a coward; even his villainy required courage. But go on."

"He died facing the enemy, and his last words were of you. He begged your forgiveness; he implored that you forget that black moment. He was young, he said; and they offered him a thousand crowns. In a moment of despair he fell."

"Despair? Did he confess to you the crime he committed?"

"Yes."

"Did he tell you to whom he sold his honor?"

"That he never knew. A Gipsy from the hills came to him, so he said.

Harold MacGrath

"From Jugendheit?"

"I say that he knew nothing. He believed that the Gipsy wanted her highness to hold for ransom. Hans spoke of a girl called Tekla."

"Tekla? Ah, yes; Hans was in love with that doll-face."

"Doll-face or not, Hans evidently loved her. She jilted him, and he did not care then what happened. His one desire was to leave Dreiberg. And this Gipsy brought the means and the opportunity."

"Not Jugendheit?"

"Who knows? Hans followed the band of Gipsies into the mountains. The real horror of his act did not come home to him till then. Ah, the remorse! But it was too late. They dressed the little one in rags. But when I ran away from them I took her little shoes and cloak and locket."

Hermann was on his feet!

Grumbach relighted his cigar which had gone out. The smoke wavered about his face and slowly ascended. His eyes were as bright and glowing as coals. He waited. He had made the slip without premeditation; but what was done was done. So he waited.

Hermann dropped his hands on the table and leaned forward.

"Is it you, Hans, and I did not know you?"

"It is I, brother."

"My God!" Hermann sank down weakly. The ceiling spun

and the gaslight separated itself into a hundred flames. "You said he was dead!"

"So I am, to the world, to you, and to all who knew me," quietly.

"Why have you returned?"

Hans shrugged. "I don't know. Perhaps I am a fool; perhaps I am willing to pay the penalty of my crime. At least that was uppermost in my mind till I learned that her highness had been found."

"Hans, Hans, the duke has sworn to hang you!"

Hans laughed. "The rope is not made that will fit my neck. Will you denounce me, brother?"

"I?" Hermann shrank back in horror.

"Why not? Five thousand crowns still hang over me."

"Blood-money for me? No, Hans!"

"Besides, I have made a will. At my death you will be rich."

"Rich?"

"Yes, Hermann. I am worth two hundred thousand crowns."

Hermann breathed with effort. So many things had beaten upon his brain in the past ten minutes that he was dazed. His brother Hans alive and here, and rich?

"But riches are not everything."

"Sometimes they are little enough," Hans agreed.

"Why did you do it?" Hermann's voice was full of agony.

"Have I not told you, Hermann? There is nothing more to be added." Then, with rising passion: "Nothing more, now that my heart is blistered and scarred with regret and remorse. God knows that I have repented and repented. I went to war because I wanted to be killed. They shot me here, and here, and here, and this saber-cut would have split the skull of any other man. But it was willed that I should come back here."

"My poor brother! You must fly from here at once!"

"From what?" tranquilly.

"The chancellor is suspicious."

"I know that. But since you, my brother, failed to identify me, certainly his excellency will not. I shall make no slip as in your case. And you will not betray me when I tell you that I have returned principally to find out whence came those thousand crowns."

"Ah! Find that out, Hans; yes, yes!" Hermann began to look more like himself. "But what was your part?"

"Mine? I was to tell where her highness and her nurse were to be at a certain hour of the day. Nothing more was necessary. My running away was the expression of my guilt; otherwise they would never have connected me with the abduction."

"Have you any suspicions?"

"None. And remember, you must not know me, Hermann, no

matter where we meet. I am sleepy." Hans rose.

And this, thought Hermann, his bewilderment gaining life once more, and this calm, unruffled man, whose hair was whiter than his own, a veteran of the bloodiest civil war in history, this prosperous mechanic, was his little brother Hans!

"Hans, have you no other greeting?" Hermann asked, spreading out his arms.

The wanderer's face beamed; and the brothers embraced.

"You forgive me, then, Hermann?"

"Must I not, little Hans? You are all that is left me of the blood. True, I swore that if ever I saw you again I should curse you."

The two stood back from each other, but with arms still entwined.

"Perhaps, Hans, I did not watch you closely enough in those days."

"And what has become of the principal cause?"

"The cause?"

"Tekla."

"Bah! She is fat and homely and the mother of seven squalling children."

"What a world! To think that Tekla should be at the bottom of all this tangle! What irony! I ruin my life, I break the heart of the grand duke, I nearly cause war between two friendly states - why? Tekla, now fat and homely and the mother of seven, would not marry me. The devil rides strange horses."

"Good night, Hans."

"Good night, Hermann, and God bless you for your forgiveness. Always come at night if you wish to see me, but do not come often; they might remark it."

A rap on the door startled them. Hans, a finger of warning on his lips, opened the door. Carmichael stood outside.

"Ah, Captain!" Hans took Carmichael by the hand and drew him into the room.

Carmichael, observing Hermann, was rather confused as to what to do.

"Good evening, Hermann," he said.

"Good evening, Herr Carmichael."

Hermann passed into the hail and softly closed the door after him. It was better that the American should not see the emotion which still illumined his face.

"What's the good word, Captain?" inquired Hans.

Carmichael put in a counter-query: "What was your brother doing here?"

"I have told him who I am."

"Was it wise?"

"Hermann sleeps soundly; he will talk neither in his sleep nor in his waking hours. He has forgiven me."

"For what?" thoughtlessly.

"The time for explanations has not yet come, Captain."

"Pardon me, Grumbach; I was not thinking. But I came to bring you the invitation to the military ball."

The broad white envelope, emblazoned with the royal arms, fascinated Hans, not by its resplendency, but by the possibilities which it afforded.

"Thank you; it was very good of you."

"It was a pleasure, comrade. What do you say to an hour or two at the Black Eagle? We'll drown our sorrows together."

"Have you any sorrows, Captain?"

"Who hasn't? Life is a patchwork with the rounding-out pieces always missing. Come along. I'm lonesome to-night."

"So am I," said Hans.

The Black Eagle was lively as usual; and there were some familiar faces. The vintner was there and so was Gretchen. Carmichael hailed her.

"This is my last night here, Herr Carmichael," she said.

"Somebody has left you a fortune?" There was a jest in Carmichael's eyes.

"Yes," replied Gretchen, her lips unsmiling.

"The poor lady who lived on the top floor of my grand-mother's house was rich. She left me a thousand crowns."

Carmichael and Grumbach: "A thousand crowns!"

"And what will you do with all that money?" asked Hans.

"I am going to study music."

"I thought you were going to be married soon," said Carmichael.

"Surely. But that will not hinder. I shall have enough for two." Gretchen saw no reason why she should tell them of the princess' generosity.

"But how does he take it?" asked Carmichael, with a motion of his head toward the vintner, half hidden behind a newspaper.

"He doesn't like the idea at all. But the Herr Direktor says that I am a singer, and that some day I shall be rich and famous."

"When that day comes I shall be there with many a brava!"

The vintner, who sat near enough to catch a bit of the conversation, scowled over the top of his paper. Carmichael eyed him mischievously. Gretchen picked up her coppers and went away.

"A beautiful girl," said Hans abstractedly. "She might be Hebe with no trouble at all."

Carmichael admired Hans. There was always some new phase in the character of this quiet and unassuming German.

A plumber who was familiar with the classics was not an ordinary person. He raised his stein and Hans extended his. After that they smoked, with a word or two occasionally in comment.

At that day there was only one newspaper in Dreiberg. It was a dry and solid sheet, of four pages, devoted to court news, sciences, and agriculture. The vintner presently smoothed down the journal, opened his knife, and cut out a paragraph. Carmichael, following his movements slyly, wondered what he had seen to interest him to the point of preservation. The vintner crushed the remains of the sheet into a ball and dropped it to the floor. Then he finished his beer, rose, and proceeded toward the stairs leading to the rathskeller below. Down these he disappeared.

An idea came to Carmichael. He called a waitress and asked her to bring a copy of that day's paper. Meantime he recovered the vintner's paper, and when he finally put the two together, it was a simple matter to replace the missing cutting. Grumbach showed a mild interest over the procedure.

"Why do you do that, Captain?"

"A little idea I have; it may not amount to anything." But the American was puzzled over the cutting. There were two sides to it: which had interested the vintner? "Do you care for another beer?"

"No, I am tired and sleepy, Captain."

"All right; we'll go back to the hotel. There is nothing going on here to-night."

But Carmichael was mistaken for once.

A little time later Herr Goldberg harangued his fellow socialists bitterly. Gretchen's business in this society was to serve. They had selected her because they knew that she inclined toward the propaganda. Few spoke to her, outside of giving orders, and then kindly.

The rathskeller had several windows and doors. These led to the *Biergarten*, to the wine-cellar, and to an alley which had no opening on the street. The police had as yet never arrested anybody; but several times the police had dispersed Herr Goldberg and his disciples on account of the noise. The window which led to the blind alley was six feet from the floor, twice as broad as it was high, and unbarred. Under this window sat the vintner. He was a probationer, a novitiate; this was his second attendance. He liked to sit in the shadow and smile at Herr Goldberg's philosophy, which, summed up briefly, meant that the rich should divide with the poor and that the poor should hang on to what they had or got. It may have never occurred to Herr Goldberg that the poor were generally poor because of their incapabilities, their ignorance, and incompetence. To-night, however, there were variety and spice with his Jeremiad.

"Brothers, shall this thing take place? Shall the daughter of Ehrenstein become Jugendheit's vassal? Oh, how we have fallen! Where is the grand duke's pride we have heard so much about? Are we, then, afraid of Jugendheit?"

"No!" roared his auditors, banging their stems and tankards. The vintner joined the demonstration, banging his stein as lustily as the next one.

"Have you thought what this marriage will cost us in taxes?"

"What?"

"Thousands of crowns, thousands! Do we not always pay for the luxuries of the rich? Do not their pleasures grind us so much deeper into the dirt? Yes, we are the corn they grind. And shall we submit, like the dogs in Flanders, to become beasts of burden?"

"No, no!"

"I have a plan, brothers; it will show the duke to what desperation he has driven us at last. We will mob the Jugendheit embassy on the day of the wedding; we will tear it apart, brick by brick, stone by stone."

"Hurrah!" cried the noisy ones. They liked talk of this order. They knew it was only here that great things happened, the division of riches and mob-rule. Beer was cheaper by the keg.

The noise subsided. Gretchen spoke.

"Her serene highness will not marry the king of Jugendheit."

Every head swung round in her direction.

"What is that you say?" demanded Herr Goldberg.

Gretchen repeated her statement. It was the first time she had ever raised her voice in the councils.

"Oh, indeed!" said Goldberg, bowing with ridicule: "Since when did her serene highness make you her confidante?"

"Her serene highness told me so herself." Gretchen's eyes, which had held only mildness and good-will, now sparkled with contempt.

A roar of laughter went up, for the majority of them thought that Gretchen was indulging in a little pleasantry.

"Ho-ho! So you are on speaking terms with her highness?" Herr Goldberg laughed.

"Is there anything strange in this fact?" she asked, keeping her tones even.

The vintner made a sign to her, but she ignored it.

"Strange?" echoed Herr Goldberg, becoming furious at having the interest in himself thus diverted. "Since when did goose-girls and barmaids become on intimate terms with her serene highness?"

Gretchen pressed the vintner's arm to hold him in his chair.

"Does not your socialism teach that we are all equal?"

The vintner thumped with his stein in approval, and others imitated him. Goldberg was no ordinary fool. He sidestepped defeat by an assumption of frankness.

"Tell us about it. If I have spoken harshly it is only reasonable. Tell us under what circumstance you met her highness and how she happened to tell you this very important news. Every one knows that this marriage is to take place."

Gretchen nodded. "Nevertheless, her highness has changed her mind." And she recounted picturesquely her adventure in the royal gardens, and all hung on her words in a kind of maze. It was all very well to shout, "Down with royalty!" it was another matter to converse and shake bands with it.

"Hurrah!" shouted the vintner. "Long live her highness!

Down with Jugendheit!"

There was a fine chorus.

And there was a fine tableau not down on the evening's program. A police officer and three assistants came down the stairs quietly.

"Let no one leave this room!" the officer said sternly.

The dramatic pause was succeeded by a babel of confusion. Chairs scraped, stems clattered, and the would-be liberators huddled together like so many sheep rounded up by a shepherd-dog.

"Ho, there! Stop him, you!"

It was the vintner who caused this cry; and the agility with which he scrambled through the window into the blind alley was an inspiration.

"After him!" yelled the officer. "He is probably the one rare bird in the bunch."

But they searched in vain.

Gretchen stared ruefully at the blank window.

Somehow this flight pained her; somehow it gave her the heartache to learn that her idol was afraid of such a thing as a policeman.

"Out into the street, every mother's son of you!" cried the officer angrily to the quaking socialists. "This is your last warning, Goldberg. The next time you go to prison for seditious teachings. Out with you!"

The socialists could not have emptied the cellar any quicker had there been a fire.

Gretchen alone remained. It was her duty to carry the steins up to the bar. The officer, rather thorough for his kind, studied the floor under the window. He found a cutting from a newspaper. This interested him.

"Do you know who this fellow was?" with a jerk of his head toward the window.

"He is Leopold Dietrich, a vintner, and we are soon to be married." There was a flaw in the usual sweetness of her voice.

"So? What made him run away like this?"

"He is new to Dreiberg. Perhaps he thought you were going to arrest every one. Oh, he has done nothing wrong; I am sure of that."

"There is one way to prove it."

"And what is that?"

"Ask him if he is not a spy from Jugendheit," roughly.

The steins clicked crisply in Gretchen's arms; one of them fell and broke at her feet.

CHAPTER XII

LOVE'S DOUBTS

Gretchen, troubled in heart and mind over the strange event of the night, walked slowly home, her head inclined, her arms swinging listlessly at her side. A spy, this man to whom she had joyously given the flower of her heart and soul? There was some mistake; there must be some mistake. She shivered; for the word spy carried with it all there was in deceit, treachery, cunning. In war time she knew that spies were necessary, that brave men took perilous hazards, without reward, without renown; but in times of peace nothing but opprobrium covered the word. A political scavenger, the man she loved? No; there was some mistake. The bit of newspaper cutting did not worry her. Anybody might have been curious about the doings of the king of Jugendheit and his uncle the prince regent. Because the king hunted in Bavaria with the crown prince, and his uncle conferred with the king of Prussia in Berlin, it did not necessarily follow that Leopold Dietrich was a spy. Gretchen was just. She would hear his defense before she judged him.

Marking the first crook in the Krumerweg was an ancient lamp hanging from the side of the wall. The candle in this lamp burned night and day, through winter's storms and summer's balms. The flame dimmed and glowed, a kindly reminder in the gloom. It was a shrine to the Virgin Mary; and before this Gretchen paused, offering a silent prayer that the Holy Mother preserve this dream of hers.

A footstep from behind caused her to start. The vintner took her roughly in his arms and kissed her many times.

Her heart shook within her, but she did not surrender her purpose under these caresses. She freed herself energetically and stood a little away from him, panting and star-eyed.

"Gretchen?"

She did not speak.

"What is it?"

"You ask?"

"Was it a crime, then, to jump out of the window?" He laughed.

Gretchen's face grew sterner. "Were you afraid?"

"For a moment. I have never run afoul the police. I thought perhaps we were all to be arrested."

"Well, and what then?"

"What then? Uncomfortable quarters in stone rooms. I preferred discretion to valor."

"Perhaps you did not care to have the police ask you questions?"

"What is all this about?" He pulled her toward him so that he could look into her eyes.

"What is the matter? Answer!"

"Are you not a spy from Jugendheit?" thinly.

He flung aside her hand. "So! The first doubt that enters your ear finds harbor there. A spy from Jugendheit; that is a police suggestion, and you believed it!"

"Do you deny it?" Gretchen was not cowed by his anger, which her own evenly matched.

"Yes," proudly, snatching his hat from his head and throwing it violently at her feet; "yes, I deny it. I am not a spy from any country; I have not sold the right to look any man in the eye."

"I have asked you many questions," she replied, "but you are always laughing. It is a pleasant way to avoid answering. I have given you my heart and all its secrets. Have you opened yours as frankly?"

To meet anger with logic and sense is the simplest way to overcome it. The vintner saw himself at bay. He stooped to recover his hat, not so much to regain it but to steal time to conjure up some way out.

"Gretchen, here under the Virgin I swear to you that I love you as a man loves but once in his life. If I were rich, I would gladly fling these riches to the wind for your sake. If I were a king, I'd barter my crown for a smile and a kiss. I have done no wrong; I have committed no crime. But you must have proof; so be it. We will go together to the police-bureau and settle this doubt once and for all."

"When?" Gretchen's heart was growing warm again.

"Now, to-night, while they are hunting for me."

"Forgive me!" brokenly.

"Come!"

"No, Leopold, this test is not necessary."

"I insist. This thing must be righted publicly."

"And I was thinking that the man I loved was a coward!"

"I am braver than you dream, Gretchen." And in truth he was, for he was about to set forth for the lion's den, and only amazing cleverness could extricate him. Man never enters upon the foolhardy unless it be to dazzle a woman. And the vintner's love for Gretchen was no passing thing. "Let us hurry; it is growing late. They will be shutting off the lights before we return."

The police-bureau was far away, but the distance was nothing to these healthy young people.

They progressed at a smart pace and in less than twenty minutes they arrived. It was Gretchen who drew back fearfully.

"After all, will it not be foolish?" she suggested.

"They will be searching for me," he answered.

"It will be easier if I present myself. It will bear testimony that I am innocent of any wrong."

"I will go in with you," determinedly.

The police officer, or, to be more particular, the sub-chief of the bureau, received them with ill-concealed surprise.

"I have learned that you are seeking me," said the vintner, taking off his cap. His yellow curls waved about his forehead in moist profusion.

Immediately the sub-chief did not know what to say. This was out of the ordinary, conspicuously so. There was little precedent by which to act in a case like this. So in order to appear that nothing could destroy his official poise, he let the two stand before his desk while he sorted some papers.

"You are not a native of Dreiberg," he began.

"No, Herr; I am from Bavaria. If you will look into your records you will find that my papers were presented two or three weeks ago."

"Let me see them."

The vintner's passports were produced. The sub-chief compared them to the corresponding number in his book. There was nothing wrong about them.

"I do not recollect seeing you here before."

"It was one of your assistants who originally went over the papers."

"What is your business?"

"I am a vintner by trade, Herr."

"And are there not plenty of vineyards in Bavaria?"

"We vintners," with an easy gesture, "are of a roving disposition. I have been all along the Rhine and the Moselle. I prefer grapes to hops."

"But why Dreiberg? The best vineyards are south."

"Who can say where we shall go next? Dreiberg seemed good enough for me," with a shy glance at Gretchen.

"Why did you jump out of the window?"

"I was frightened at first, Herr. I did not know that you merely dispersed meetings. I believed that we were all to be arrested. Such measures are in force in Munich."

"You accused him of being a Jugendheit spy," broke in Gretchen, who was growing impatient under these questions, which seemed to go nowhere in particular.

"You be silent," warned the sub-chief.

"I am here because of that accusation," said the vintner.

"What have you to say?"

"I deny it."

"That is easy to do. But can you prove it?"

"It is for you to prove, Herr."

"Read this."

It was the cutting. The vintner read it, his brows drawn

together in a puzzled frown. He turned the slip over carelessly. The sub-chief's eyes bored into him like gimlets.

"I can make nothing of this, Herr. When I cut this out of the paper it was to preserve the notice on the other side." The vintner returned the cutting.

The sub-chief read aloud:

"Vintners and presses and pruners wanted for the season. Find and liberal compensation. Apply, Holtz."

Gretchen laughed joyously; the vintner grinned; the sub-chief swore under his breath.

"The devil fly away with you both!" he cried, making the best of his chagrin. "And when you marry, don't invite me to the wedding."

After they had gone, however, he called for an assistant.

"Did you see that young vintner?"

"Yes."

"Follow him, night and day. Find out where he lives and what he does; and ransack his room if possible. He is either an innocent man or a sleek rascal. Report to me this time each night."

"And the girl?"

"Don't trouble about her. She is under the patronage of her serene highness. She's as right as a die. It's the man. He was too easy; he didn't show enough concern. An ordinary vintner would have been frightened. This fellow smiled."

"And if I find out anything suspicious?"

"Arrest him out of hand and bring him here at once."

Alone once more the sub-chief studied the cutting with official thoroughness. He was finally convinced, by the regularity of the line on the printed side as compared with the irregularity of the line on the advertising side, that the vintner had lied. And yet there was no proof that he had.

"This young fellow will go far," he mused, with reluctant admiration.

On reaching the street Gretchen gave rein to her laughter. What promised to be a tragedy was only a farce. The vintner laughed, too, but Momus would have criticized his laughter.

The night was not done yet; there were still some more surprises in store for the vintner. As they turned into the Krumerweg they almost ran into Carmichael. What was the American consul doing in this part of the town, so near midnight? Carmichael recognized them both. He lifted his hat, but the vintner cavalierly refused to respond.

"Herr Carmichael!" said Gretchen. "And what are you doing here this time of the night?"

"I have been on a fool's errand," urbanely.

"And who sent you?"

"The god of fools himself, I guess. I am looking for a kind of ghost, a specter in black that leaves the palace early in the evening and returns late, whose destination has invariably been forty Krumerweg."

The vintner started.

"My house?" cried Gretchen.

"Yours? Perhaps you can dispel this phantom?" said Carmichael.

Gretchen was silent.

"Oh! You know something. Who is she?"

"A lady who comes on a charitable errand. But now she will come no more."

"And why not?"

"The object of her visits is gone," Gretchen answered sadly.

"My luck!" exclaimed Carmichael ruefully.

"I am always building houses of cards. I don't suppose I shall ever reform."

"Are you not afraid to walk about in this part of the town so late?" put in the vintner, who was impatient to be gone.

"Afraid? Of what? Thieves? Bah, my little man, I carry a sword-stick, and moreover I know how to use it tolerably well. Good night." And he swung along easily, whistling an air from *The Barber of Seville.*

The insolence in Carmichael's tone set the vintner's ears a-burning, but he swallowed his wrath.

"I like him," Gretchen declared, as she stopped before the house.

Harold MacGrath

"Why?" jealously.

"Because he is always like that; pleasant, never ruffled, kindly. He will make a good husband to some woman."

The vintner shrugged. He was not patient to-night.

"Who is this mysterious woman?"

"I am not free to tell you."

"Oh!"

"Leopold, what is the matter with you to-night? You act like a boy."

"Perhaps the police muddle is to blame. Besides, every time I see this man Carmichael I feel like a baited dog."

"In Heaven's name, why?"

"Nothing that I can remember. But I have asked you a question."

"And I have declined to answer that question. All my secrets are yours, but this one is another's."

"Is it her highness?"

Gretchen fingered the latch suggestively.

"I am wrong, Gretchen; you are right. Kiss me!"

She liked the tone; she liked the kisses, too, though they hurt.

"Good night, my man!" she whispered.

"Good night, my woman! To-morrow night at eight."

He turned and ran lightly and swiftly up the street. Gretchen remained standing in the doorway till she could see him no more. Why should he run like that? She raised the latch and went inside.

From the opposite doorway a mountaineer, a carter, a butcher, and a baker stepped cautiously forth.

"He heard something," said the mountaineer. "He has ears like a rat for hearing. What a pretty picture!" cynically. "All the world loves a lover - sometimes. Touching scene!"

No one replied; no one was expected to reply; more than that, no one cared to court the fury which lay thinly disguised in the mountaineer's tones.

"To-morrow night; you heard what he said. I am growing weary of this play. You will stop him on his way to yonder house. A closed carriage will be at hand. Before he enters, remember. She watches him too long when he leaves. Fool!"

The quartet stole along in the darkness, noiselessly and secretly.

The vintner had indeed heard something. He knew not what this noise was, but it was enough to set his heels to flying. A phase had developed in his character that defied analysis; suspicion, suspicion of daylight, of night, of shadows moving by walls, of footsteps behind. Only a little while ago he had walked free-hearted and careless. This growing habit of skulking was gall and wormwood. Once in his room, which was directly over the office of the American consulate, he fell into a chair, inert and breathless. What a night! What a series of adventures!

"Only a month ago I was a boy. I am a man now, for I know what it is to suffer. Gretchen, dear Gretchen, I am a black scoundrel! But if I break your heart I shall break my own along with it. I wonder how much longer it will last. But for that vintner's notice I should have been lost."

By and by he lighted a candle. The room held a cot, a table, and two chairs. The vintner's wardrobe consisted of a small pack thrown carelessly into a corner. Out of the drawer in the table he took several papers and burned them. The ashes he cast out of the window. He knew something about police methods; they were by no means all through with him. Ah! A patch of white paper, just inside the door, caught his eye. He fetched it to the candle. What he read forced the color from his cheeks and his hands were touched with transient palsy.

"The devil! What shall I do now?" he muttered, thoroughly dismayed.

What indeed should he do? Which way should he move? How long had *he* been in Dreiberg? Ah, that would be rich! What a joke! It would afford him a smile in his old age. Carmichael, Carmichael! The vintner chuckled softly as he scribbled this note:

"If Herr Carmichael would learn the secret of number forty Krumerweg, let him attire himself as a vintner and be in the Krumerweg at eight o'clock to-night."

"So there is a trap, and I am to beware of a mountaineer, a carter, a butcher, and a baker? Thanks, Scharfenstein, my friend, thanks! You are watching over me."

He blew out his candle and went to bed.

CHAPTER XIII

A DAY DREAM

Colonel Von Wallenstein curled his mustaches. It was a happy thought that had taken him into the Adlergasse. This Gretchen had been haunting his dreams, and here she was, coming into his very arms, as it were. The sidewalk was narrow. Gretchen, casually noting that an officer stood in the way, sensibly veered into the road. But to her surprise the soldier left the sidewalk and planted himself in the middle of the road. There was no mistaking this second maneuver. The officer, whom she now recognized, was bent on intercepting her. She stopped, a cold fury in her heart.

To make sure, she essayed to go round. It was of no use. So she stopped again.

"Herr," she said quietly, "I wish to pass."

"That is possible, Gretchen."

It was nine o'clock in the morning. The Adlergasse was at this time deserted.

"Will you stand aside?"

"You have been haunting my dreams, Gretchen."

"That would be a pity. But I wish to pass."

"Presently. Do you know that you are the most beautiful being in all Dreiberg?"

"I am in a hurry," said Gretchen.

"There is plenty of time."

"Not to listen to foolish speeches."

"I am not going to let you pass till I have had a kiss."

"Ah!" Battle flamed up in Gretchen's eyes. Somewhere in the past, in some remote age, her forebears had been men-at-arms or knights in the crusades.

"You are very hard to please. Some women - "

"But what kind of women?" bitingly. "Not such as I should care to meet. Will you let me by peacefully?"

"After the toll, after the toll!"

Too late she started to run. He laughed and caught hold of her. Slowly but irresistibly he drew her toward his heart. The dead-white of her face should have warned him. With a supreme effort she freed herself and struck him across the face; and there was a man's strength in the flat of her hand. Quick as a flash she whirled round and ran up the street, he hot upon her heels. He was raging now with pain and chagrin. The one hope for Gretchen now lay in the Black Eagle; and into the tavern she darted excitedly.

"Fraeu Bauer," she cried, gasping as much in wrath as for lack of breath, "may I come behind your counter?"

"To be sure, child. Whatever is the matter?"

Wallenstein's entrance was answer sufficient. His hand, held against his stinging cheek, was telltale enough for the proprietress of the Black Eagle.

"Shame!" she cried. She knew her rights. She was not afraid to speak plainly to any officer in the duchy, however high he might be placed.

"I can not get at you there, Gretchen," said the colonel, giving to his voice that venom which the lady's man always has at hand when thwarted in his gallantries. "You will have to come hence presently."

"She shall stay here all day," declared Fraeu Bauer decidedly.

"I can wait." The colonel, now possessing two smarts, one to his cheek and one to his vanity, made for the door. But there was a bulk in the doorway formidable enough to be worth serious contemplation.

"What is going on here, little goose-girl?" asked the grizzled old man, folding his arms round his oak staff.

"Herr Colonel insulted me."

"Insulted you?" The colonel laughed boisterously. This was good; an officer insult a wench of this order! "Out of the way!" he snarled at the obstruction in the doorway.

"What did he try to do to you, Gretchen?"

"He tried to kiss me!"

"The man who tries to kiss a woman against her will is always at heart a coward," said the mountaineer.

The colonel seized the old man by the shoulder to push him aside. The other never so much as stirred. He put out one of his arms and clasped the colonel in such a manner that he gasped. He was in the clutch of a Carpathian bear.

"Well, my little soldier?" said the mountaineer, his voice even and not a vein showing in his neck.

"I will kill you for this!" breathed the colonel heavily.

"So?" The old man thrust him back several feet, without any visible exertion. He let his staff slide into his hand.

The moment the colonel felt himself liberated, he drew his saber and lunged toward his assailant. There was murder in his heart. The two women screamed. The old man laughed. He turned the thrust with his staff. The colonel, throwing caution to the four winds, surrendered to his rage. He struck again. The saber rang against the oak. This dexterity with the staff carried no warning to the enraged officer. He struck again and again. Then the old man struck back. The pain in the colonel's arm was excruciating. His saber rattled to the stone flooring. Before he could recover the weapon the victor had put his foot upon it. He was still smiling, as if the whole affair was a bit of pastime.

On his part the colonel's blood suddenly cooled. This was no accident; this meddling peasant had at some time or other held a saber in his hand and knew how to use it famously well. The colonel realized that he had played the fool nicely.

"My sword," he demanded, with as much dignity as he could muster.

"Will you sheathe it?" the old man asked mildly.

"Since it is of no particular use," bitterly.

"I could have broken it half a dozen times. Here, take it. But be wise in the future, and draw it only in the right."

The gall was bitter on the colonel's tongue, but his head was evenly balanced now. He jammed the blade into the scabbard.

"I should like a word or two with you outside," said the mountaineer.

"To what purpose?"

"To a good one, as you will learn."

The two of them went out. Gretchen, overcome, fell upon Fraeu Bauer's neck and wept soundly. The whole affair had been so sudden and appalling.

Outside the old man laid his hand on the colonel's arm.

"You must never bother her again."

"Must?"

"The very word. Listen, and do not be a fool because you have some authority on the general staff. You are Colonel von Wallenstein; you are something more besides."

"What do you infer?"

"I infer nothing. Now and then there happens strange leakage in the duke's affairs. The man is well paid. He is a gambler, and one is always reasonably certain that the gambler will be wanting money. Do you begin to understand me, or must I be more explicit?"

"Who are you?"

"Who I am is of no present consequence. But I know who and *what* you are. That is all-sufficient. If you behave yourself in the future, you will be allowed to continue in prosperity. But if you attempt to molest that girl again and I hear of it, there will be no more gold coming over the frontier from Jugendheit. Now, do you understand?"

"Yes." The colonel experienced a weakness in the knees.

"Go. But be advised and walk circumspectly." The speaker showed his back insolently, and reentered the Black Eagle.

The colonel, pale and distrait, stared at the empty door; and he saw in his mind's eye a squad of soldiers, a wall, a single volley, and a dishonored roll of earth. Military informers were given short shrift. It was not a matter of tearing off orders and buttons; it was death. Who was this terrible old man, with the mind of a serpent and the strength of a bear? The colonel went to the barracks, but his usual debonair was missing.

"I am going into the garden, Gretchen. Bring me a stein of brown." The mountaineer smiled genially.

"But I am not working here any more," said Gretchen.

"No?"

"She has had a fortune left her," said Fraeu Bauer.

"Well, well!" The mountaineer seemed vastly pleased. "And how much is this fortune?"

"Two thousand crowns." Gretchen was not sure, but to her there always seemed to be a secret laughter behind those clear eyes.

"Handsome! And what will you do now?"

"She is to study for the opera."

"Did I not prophesy it?" he cried jubilantly.

"Did I not say that some impresario would discover you and make your fortune?"

"There is plenty of work ahead," said Gretchen sagely.

"Always, no matter what we strive for. But a brave heart and a cheerful smile carry you half-way up the hill. Where were you going when this popinjay stopped you?"

"I was going to the clock-mender's for a clock he is repairing."

"I've nothing to do. I'll go with you. I've an idea that I should like to talk with you about a very important matter. Perhaps it would be easier to talk first and then go for the clock. If you have it you'll be watching it. Will you come into the garden with me now?"

"Yes, Herr." Gretchen would have gone anywhere with this strange man. He inspired confidence.

The garden was a snug little place; a few peach-trees and arbor-vines and vegetables, and tables and chairs on the brick walk.

"So you are going to become a prima donna?" he began, seating himself opposite her.

"I am going to try," she smiled. "What is it you wish to say to me?"

"I am wondering how to begin," looking at the blue sky.

"Is it difficult?"

"Yes, very."

"Then why bother?"

"Some things are written before we are born. And I must, in the order of things, read this writing to you."

"Begin," said Gretchen.

"Have you any dreams?"

"Yes," vaguely.

"I mean the kind one has in the daytime, the dreams when the eyes are wide open."

"Oh, yes!"

"Who has not dreamed of riding in carriages, of dressing in silks, of wearing rich ornaments?"

"Ah!" Gretchen clasped her hands and leaned on her elbows.

"And there are palaces, too."

"To be sure." There was a long pause. "How would you like a dream of this kind to come true?"

"Do they ever come true?"

"In this particular case, I am a fairy. I know that I do not look it; still, I am. With one touch of my wand - this oak staff - I can bring you all these things you have dreamed about."

"But what would I do with carriages and jewels? I am only a goose-girl, and I am to be married."

"To that young rascal of a vintner?"

"He is not a rascal!" loyally.

"It will take but little to make him one," with an odd grimness.

Gretchen did not understand.

He resumed, "how would you like a little palace, with servants at your beck and call, with carriages to ride in, with silks and velvets to wear, and jewels to adorn your hair? How would you like these things? Eh? Never again to worry about your hands, never again to know the weariness of toil, to be mistress of swans instead of geese?"

A shadow fell upon Gretchen's face; the eagerness died out of her eyes.

"I do not understand you, Herr. By what right should I possess these things?"

Harold MacGrath

"By the supreme right of beauty, beauty alone."

"Would it be - honest?"

For the first time he lowered his eyes. The clear crystal spirit in hers embarrassed him.

"Come, let us go for your clock," he said, rising. "I am an old fool. I forgot that one talks like this only to opera-dancers."

Then Gretchen understood. "I am all alone," she said; "I have had to fight my battles with these two hands."

"I am a black devil, *Kindchen*. Forget what I have said. You are worthy the brightest crown in Europe; but you wear a better one than that - goodness. If any one should ever make you unhappy, come to me. I will be your godfather. Will you forgive an old man who ought to have known better?"

There was such unmistakable honesty in his face and eyes that she did not hesitate, but placed her hand in his.

"Why did you ask all those questions?" she inquired.

"Perhaps it was only to test your strength. You are a brave and honest girl."

"And if trouble came," now smiling, "where should I find you?"

"I shall be near when it comes. Good fairies are always close at hand." He swept his hat from his head; ease and grace were in the movement; no irony, nothing but respect. "And do you love this vintner?"

"With all my heart."

"And he loves you?"

"Yes. His lips might lie, but not his eyes and the touch of his hand."

"So much the worse!" said the mountaineer inaudibly.

Gretchen had gone home with her clock; but still Herr Ludwig, as the mountaineer called himself, tarried in the dim and dusty shop. Clocks, old and new, broken and whole, clocks from the four ends of the world; and watches, thick and clumsy, thin and graceful, of gold and silver and pewter.

"Is there anything you want?" asked the clock-mender.

Herr Ludwig turned. How old this clock-mender was, how very old!

"Yes," he said. "I've a watch I should like you to look over." And he carelessly laid the beautiful time-piece on the worn wooden counter.

The clock-mender literally pounced upon it. "Where did you get a watch like this?" he demanded suspiciously.

"It is mine. You will find my name engraved inside the back lid."

The clock-mender pried open the case, adjusted his glass - and dropped it, shaking with terror.

"You?" he whispered.

"Sh!" said Herr Ludwig, putting a finger to his lips.

CHAPTER XIV

FIND THE WOMAN

The watch, slipping from the clock-mender's hand, spun like a coin on the counter, while the clock-mender himself, his eyes bulging, his jaw dangling, it might be said, staggered back upon his stool.

"So this is the end?" he said in a kind of mutter.

"The end of what?" demanded the owner of the watch.

"Of all my labors, to me and to what little I have left!"

"Fiddlesticks! I am here for no purpose regarding you, my comrade. So far as I am concerned, your secret is as dead as it ever was. I had a fancy that you were living in Paris."

"Paris! *Gott!* For seventeen, eighteen years I have traveled hither and thither, always on some false clue. Never a band of Gipsies I heard of that I did not seek them out. Nothing, nothing! You will never know what I have gone through, and uselessly, to prove my innocence. It always comes back in a circle; what benefit to me would have been a crime like that of which I was accused? Was I not high in honor? Was I not wealthy? Was not my home life a happy one? What benefit to me, I say?" a growing fierceness in his voice and gestures. "All my estates confiscated, my wife dead of shame, and I molding among these clocks!"

"But why the clocks?" in wonder.

"It was a pastime of mine when I was a boy. I used to be tinkering among all the clocks in the house. So I bought out this old shop. From time to time I have left it in the hands of an assistant. The grand duke has a wonderful Friesian clock. One day it fell out of order, and the court jeweler could do nothing with it. I was summoned, I! No one recognized me, I have changed so. I mended the clock and went away."

"But what is the use of all this, now that her highness is found?"

"My honor; to the duke it is black as ever."

"Have you gone forward any?"

"Like Sisyphus! I had begun to give up hope, when the Gipsy I was seeking was seen by one of my agents. He alone knows the secret. And I am waiting, waiting. But you believe, Ludwig?"

"Carl, you are as innocent of it all as I am or as my brother was. Come with me to Jugendheit."

"No, Ludwig, this is my country, however unjustly it has treated me."

"Yes, yes. And to think that you and I and the grand duke were comrades at Heidelberg! But if your Gipsy fails you?"

"Still I shall remain. This will be all I shall have, these

clocks. I am only sixty-eight, yet no one would believe me under eighty. I no longer gaze into mirrors. I have forgotten how I look. There were letters found in my desk, all forgeries, I knew, but so cleverly done I could only deny. I saw that my case was hopeless, so I fled to Paris. I wrote Herbeck once while there. He believed that I was innocent. I have his letter yet. He has a great heart, Ludwig, and he has done splendid work for Ehrenstein."

"He keeps a steady hand on the duke."

"But you, what are you doing in Dreiberg, in this guise?"

Herr Ludwig sat upon the counter and clasped a knee. "Do you care for fairy-stories?"

"Sometimes."

"Well, once upon a time there lived a king. He was young. He had an uncle who watched over him and his affairs. They call such uncles prince regents. This prince regent had an idea regarding the future welfare of this nephew. He would bring him up to be a man, well educated, broad-minded, and clean-lived. He should have a pilot to guide him past the traps and vices which befall the young. Time wore on. The lad grew up, clean in mind, strong in body, liberal; a fine prince. No scandalous entanglements; no gaming; no wine-bibbing beyond what any decent man may do. In his palace few saw anything of him after his fifteenth year. He went into the world under an assumed name. By and by he came home, quietly. His uncle was proud of him, for his eye was clear and his tongue was clean. In one month he was to be coronated. And now what do you think? He must have one more adventure, just one. Would his uncle go with him? Certainly not. Moreover, the time for adventure was over. He must no longer wander about; he was a king; he must put his hand to king-craft. And one morning his uncle found him gone, gone as completely as if he had never existed. What to do? Ah! The prince regent set it going that his majesty had gone a-hunting in Bavaria. Then the prince regent put on some old clothes and went a-venturing himself."

"And the end?"

"God knows!" said Ludwig, sliding off the counter.

Nothing but the ticking of the clocks was heard.

"And fatuous fool that this uncle was, he committed an almost irreparable blunder. He tried to marry his nephew."

"I understand. But if you are discovered here?"

"That is not likely."

"Ah, Ludwig, it is not the expected that always happens. Be careful; you know the full wording of Herbeck's treaty."

"Herbeck; there's a man," said Herr Ludwig admiringly. "To have found her highness as he did!"

"He is lucky," but without resentment.

The other picked up his watch. "Can I be of material assistance?"

"I want nothing," haughtily.

"Proud old imbecile!" replied the mountaineer kindly. "You have been deeply wronged, but some day you will pick up the thread in the labyrinth, and there will be light forward. I myself shall see what can be done with the duke."

"He will never be brought to reason unless indubitable evidence of my innocence confronts him. With the restoration of the princess fifty political prisoners were given their liberty and restored to citizenship. The place once occupied by my name is still blank, obliterated. It is hard. I have given the best of my heart and of my brain to Ehrenstein - for this! I am innocent."

"I believe you, Carl. Remember, Jugendheit will always welcome you. I must be going. I have much to do between now and midnight. The good God will unravel the snarl."

"Or forget it," cynically. "Good-by, Ludwig."

There was a hand-clasp, and the mountaineer took himself off. The clock-mender philosophically reached for his tools. He had wasted time enough over retrospection; he determined to occupy himself with the present only. Tick-tock! tick-tock! sang the clocks about him. All at once a volume of musical sounds broke forth; cuckoo-calls, chimes, tinkles light and thin, booms deep and vibrant. But the clock-mender bent over his work; all he was conscious of was the eternal tick-tock! tick-tock! on and on, without cessation.

* * * * *

Carmichael walked his horse. This morning he had ridden out almost to the frontier and was now on his return. As he passed through the last grove of pines and came into the clearing the picture was exquisite; the three majestic bergs of ice and snow above Dreiberg, the city shining white and fairylike in the mid-morning's sun, and the long, half-circling ribbon of a road. He sighed, and the horse cocked his ears at the sound.

No longer did Carmichael take the south pass for his

morning rides. That was the favored going of her highness, and he avoided her now. In truth, he dared not meet her now; it would have been out of wisdom. So long as she had been free his presence had caused no comment, only tolerant amusement among the nobles at court. It chafed him to be regarded as a harmless individual, for he knew that he was far from being in that class. There was a wild strain in him. Dreiberg might have waked up some fine morning to learn that for a second time her princess had been stolen, and that there was a vacancy in the American consulate. How many times had he been seized with the mad desire to snatch the bridle of her horse and ride away with her into a far country! How often had his arms started out toward her, only to drop stiffly to his sides!

March hares! They were Solons as compared with his own futile madness. But it was different now. She was to marry the king of Jugendheit; it was in the order of things that he ride alone. He knew that court etiquette demanded the isolation of the Princess Hildegarde from male escort other than that formally provided. The two soldiers detailed to act as her grooms or bodyguards were not, of course, to be considered. So, of the morning, he went down to the military field to watch the maneuvers, which were drawing to a close; or rode out to the frontier, or took the side road to Eissen, where the summer palaces were. But it was all dreary; the zest of living had somehow dropped out of things.

The road to Eissen began about six miles north of the base of the Dreiberg mountain. It swerved to the east. As Carmichael reached the fork his horse began to limp. He jumped down and removed the stone. It was then that he heard the far-off mutter of hoofs. Coming along the road from Eissen were a trio of riders. Carmichael laughed weakly.

"I swear to Heaven that this is no fault of mine!"

Harold MacGrath

Should he mount and be off before she made the turn? Bah! It was an accident; he would make the most of it. The bodyguard could easily vindicate him, in any event. He remounted and waited.

She came in full flight, rosy, radiant, as lovely as Diana. Carmichael swung his cap boyishly; and there was a swirl of dust as she drew up.

"Good morning, Herr Carmichael!"

"Good morning, your Highness!"

"Which way have you been riding?"

"Toward Jugendheit."

"And you are returning?" With a short nod of her head she signaled for the two soldiers to fall back.

The two looked at each other embarrassedly.

"Pardon, Highness," said one of them, "but the orders of the duke will not permit us to leave you. There have been thieves along the road of late."

Thieves? This was the first time Carmichael had heard of it. The real significance of the maneuver escaped him; but her highness was not fooled.

"Very well," she replied. "One of you ride forward and one of you take the rear." Then she spoke to Carmichael in English.

The soldiers shrugged. To them it did not matter what language her highness adopted so long as they obeyed the letter of the duke's instructions. The little cavalcade directed its course toward the city.

"You have not been riding of late," she said.

Then she had missed him. Carmichael's heart expanded. To be missed is to be regretted, and one regrets only those in whom one is interested.

"I have ridden the same as usual, your Highness; only I have taken this road for a change."

"Ah!" She patted the glistening neck of her mare. So he had purposely tried to avoid her? Why? She stole a sly glance at him. Why were not kings molded in this form? All the kings she had met had something the matter with them, crooked legs, weak eyes, bald, young, or old, and daft over gaming-tables and opera-dancers. And the one man among them all - at least she had been informed that the king of Jugendheit was all of a man - had politely declined. There was some chagrin in this for her, but no bitterness or rancor. In truth, she was more chagrined on her father's account than on her own.

"You should have taken the south pass. It was lovely yesterday."

"Perhaps this way has been wisest."

"Are you become afraid of me?" archly.

"Yes, your Highness." If he had looked at her instead of his horse's ears, and smiled, all would have been well.

She instantly regretted the question. "I am sorry that I have become an ogress."

"To me your highness is the most perfect of women. I am guilty of lese-majesty."

"I shall not lock you up," she said, and added under her breath, "as my good father would like to! Besides," she continued aloud, "I rather like to set the court by the ears. Whoever heard of a serene highness doing the things I do? I suppose it is because I have known years of freedom, freedom of action, of thought, of speech. These habits can not change at once. In fact, I do not believe they ever will. But the duke, my father, is good; he understands and trusts me. Ah, but I shall lead some king a merry life!" with a wicked gleam in her eyes.

"Frederick of Jugendheit?"

"Is it true that you have not heard yet? I have declined the honor."

"Your highness?"

"My serene highness," with a smile. "This, of course, is as yet a state secret; and my reason for telling you is not a princess', but a woman's. Solve it if you can."

Carmichael fumbled the reins blindly. "They say that he is a handsome young man."

"What has that to do with it? The interest he takes in his kingdom is positively negative. I have learned that he has been to his capital but twice since he was fifteen. He is even now absent on a hunting trip in Bavaria, and his coronation but a few days off. There will be only one king in Jugendheit, and that will be the prince regent."

"He has done tolerably well up to the present," observed

Carmichael, welcoming this change. "Jugendheit is prosperous; it has a splendid army. The prince regent is a fine type of man, they say, rugged, patient, frugal and sensible."

"There is an instance where he made a cruel blunder."

"No man is infallible," said he, wondering what this blunder was.

"I suppose not. Look! The artillery is firing."

Boom-boom! They saw the smoke leap from the muzzles of the cannon, and it seemed minutes before the sound reached them.

"I have a fine country, too," she said, with pride; "prosperous, and an army not inferior to that of Jugendheit."

"I was not making comparisons, your Highness."

"I know that, my friend. I was simply speaking from the heart. But I doubt if the prince regent is a better man than our Herbeck."

"I prefer Herbeck, never having met the prince regent. But I have some news for your highness."

"News for me?"

"Yes. I am about to ask for my recall," he said, the idea having come into his mind at that precise moment.

"Your recall?"

Had he been looking at her he would have noticed that the color on her fair cheeks had gone a shade lighter.

"Yes."

"Is not this sudden? it is not very complimentary to Ehrenstein."

"The happiest days in my life have been spent here."

"Then why seek to be recalled?"

"I am essentially a man of action, your Highness. I am growing dull and stupid amid these charming pleasures. Action; I have always been mixed up in some trouble or other. Here it is a round of pleasure from day to day. I long for buffets. I am wicked enough to wish for war."

"*Cherchez la femme!*" she cried. "There is a woman?"

"Oh, yes!" recklessly.

"Then go to her, my friend, go to her." And she waved her crop over his head as in benediction. "Some day, before you go, I shall ask you all about her." Ah, as if she did not know! But half the charm in life is playing with hidden dangers.

He did not speak, but caught up the reins firmly. She touched her mare on the flank, and the four began trotting, a pace which they maintained as far as the military field. Here they paused, for the scene was animated and full of color. Squadrons of cavalry raced across the field; infantry closed in or deployed; artillery rumbled, wheeled, stopped, unlimbered. Bang-bang! The earth shivered and rocked. Guerdons were flying, bugles were blowing, and sabers were flashing.

"It is beautiful," she cried, "this mimic war."

"May your highness never see aught else!" he replied fervently.

"Yes, yes; you have seen it divested of all its pomp. You have seen it in all its cruelty and horror."

"I have known even the terror of it."

"You were afraid?"

"Many times."

She laughed. It is only the coward who denies fear.

He would certainly ask for his recall or transfer. He was eating his heart out here in Dreiberg.

They began the incline. She did most of the talking, brightly and gaily; but his ears were dull, for the undercurrent passed by him. He was, for the first time, impressed with the fact that the young ladies of the court never accompanied her on her morning rides. There were frequent afternoon excursions, when several ladies and gentlemen rode with her highness, but in the mornings, never.

"Will you return to America?" she queried.

"I shall idle in Paris for a while. I have an idea that there will be war one of these days."

"And which side will you take?"

"I should be a traitor if I fought for France; I should be an ingrate if I fought against her. I should be a spectator, a neutral."

"That would expose you to danger without the right to strike a blow in defense."

"If I were hurt it would be but an accident. War correspondents would run a hundred more risks than I. Oh, I should be careful; I know war too well not to be."

"All this is strange talk for a man who is a confessed lover."

"Pardon me!" his eyes rather empty.

"Why, you tell me there is a woman; and all your talk is about war and danger. These are opposites; please explain."

"There is a woman, but she will not hinder me in any way. She will, in fact, know nothing about it."

"You are a strange lover. I never read anything like you in story-books. Forgive me! I am thoughtless. The subject may be painful to you."

The horses began to pull. Under normal circumstances Carmichael would not have dismounted, but his horse had carried him many miles that morning, and he was a merciful rider. In the war days often had his life depended upon the care of his horse.

"You have been riding hard?"

"No, only far."

"I do not believe that there is a finer horseman in all Ehrenstein than yourself."

"Your highness is very good to say that." Why had he not gone on instead of waiting at the fork?

Within a few hundred yards of the gates he mounted again. And then he saw a lonely figure sitting on the parapet. He would have recognized that square form anywhere. And he welcomed the sight of it.

"Your Highness, do you see that man yonder, on the parapet? We fought in the same cavalry. He is covered with scars. Not one man in a thousand would have gone through what he did and lived."

"Is he an American?"

"By adoption. And may I ask a favor of your highness?"

"Two!" merrily.

"May I present him? It will be the joy of his life."

"Certainly. All brave men interest me."

Grumbach rose up, uncovered, thinking that the riders were going to pass him. But to his surprise his friend Carmichael stopped his horse and beckoned to him.

"Herr Grumbach," said Carmichael, "her serene highness desires me to present you."

Hans was stricken dumb. He knew of no greater honor.

"Mr. Carmichael," she said in English, "tells me that you fought with him in the American war?"

"Yes, Highness."

She plied him with a number of questions; how many battles they had fought in, how many times they had been wounded,

Harold MacGrath

how they lived in camp, and so forth; and which was the more powerful engine of war, the infantry or the cavalry.

"The cavalry, Highness," said Hans, without hesitation.

She laughed. "If you had been a foot-soldier, you would have said the infantry; of the artillery, you would have sworn by the cannon."

"That is true, Highness. The three arms are necessary, but there is ever the individual pride in the arm one serves in."

"And that is right. You speak good English," she remarked.

"I have lived more than sixteen years in America, Highness."

"Do you like it there?"

"It is a great country, full of great ideas and great men, Highness."

"And you will go back?"

"Soon, Highness."

The mare, knowing that this was the way home, grew restive and began prancing and pawing the road. She reined in quickly. As she did so, something yellow flashed downward and tinkled as it struck the ground. Grumbach hastened forward.

"My locket," said her highness anxiously.

"It is not broken, Highness," said Grumbach; "only the chain has come apart." Then he handed it to her gravely.

"Thank you!" Her highness put both chain and locket into a small purse which she carried in her belt, touched the mare, and sped up the road, Carmichael following.

Grumbach returned to the parapet. He followed them till they passed out of sight beyond the gates.

"*Gott!*" he murmured.

His face was as livid as the scar on his head.

CHAPTER XV

THE WRONG MAN

Herbeck dropped his quill, and there was a dream in his eyes. His desk was littered with papers, well covered with ink; flowing sentences, and innumerable figures. He was the watch-dog of the duchy. Never a bill from the Reichstag that did not pass under his cold eye before it went to the duke for his signature, his approval, or veto. Not a copper was needlessly wasted, and never was one held back unnecessarily. Herbeck was just both in great and little things. The commoners could neither fool nor browbeat him.

The dream in his eyes grew; it was tender and kindly. The bar of sunlight lengthened across his desk, and finally passed on. Still he sat there, motionless, rapt. And thus the duke found him. But there was no dream in *his* eyes; they were cold with implacable anger. He held a letter in his hand and tossed it to Herbeck.

"I shall throw ten thousand men across the frontier to-night, let the consequences be what they may."

"Ten thousand men?" The dream was shattered. War again?

"Read that. It is the second anonymous communication I

have received within a week. As the first was truthful, there is no reason to believe this one to be false."

Herbeck read, and he was genuinely startled.

"What do you say to that?" triumphantly.

"This," with that rapid decision which made him the really great tactician he was. "Let them go quietly back to Jugendheit."

"No!" blazed the duke.

"Are we rich enough for war?"

"Always questions, questions! What the devil is my army for if not to uphold my dignity? Herbeck, you shall not argue me out of this."

"Rather let me reason. This is some prank, which I am sure does not concern Ehrenstein in the least. They would never dare enter Dreiberg for aught else. There must be a flaw in our secret service."

"Doubtless."

"I have seen this writing before," said Herbeck. "I shall make it my business to inquire who it is that takes this kindly interest in the affairs of state."

The duke struck the bell violently.

"Summon the chief of the police," he said to the secretary.

"Yes, yes, your Highness, let it be a police affair. This letter does not state the why and wherefore of their presence here."

"It holds enough for me."

"Will your highness leave the matter in my hands?"

"Herbeck, in some things you are weak."

"And in others I am strong," smiled the chancellor. "I am weak when there is talk of war; I am strong when peace is in the balance."

"Is it possible, Herbeck, that you do not appreciate the magnitude of the situation?"

"It is precisely because I do that I wish to move slowly. Wait. Let the police find out *why* they are here. There will be time enough then to declare war. They have never seen her highness. Who knows?"

"Ah! But they have violated the treaty."

"That depends upon whether their presence here is or is not a menace to the state. If they are here on private concerns which in no wise touch Ehrenstein, it would be foolhardy to declare war. Your highness is always letting your personal wounds blur your eyesight. Some day you will find that Jugendheit is innocent."

"God hasten the day and hour!"

"Yes, let us hope that the mystery of it all will be cleared up. You are just and patient in everything but this." Herbeck idled with his quill. The little finger of his right hand was badly scarred, the mutilation of a fencing-bout in his student days.

"What do you advise?" wearily. It seemed to the duke that

Herbeck of late never agreed with him.

"My advice is to wait. In a day or so arrest them under the pretext that you believe them to be spies. If they remain mute, then the case is serious, and you will have them on the hip. If, on the other hand, this invasion is harmless and they declare themselves, the matter can be adjusted in this wise: ignore their declaration and confine them a day or two in the city prison, then publish the news broadcast. Having themselves broken the letter if not the spirit of the treaty, they will not dare declare war. Every court in Europe will laugh."

The duke struck his hands together. "You are always right, Herbeck. This plan could not have been devised better or more to my satisfaction." The duke laughed. "You are right. Ah, here is the chief."

Herbeck read the letter in part to the chief, who jotted down the words, repeating aloud in a kind of mutter: "A mountaineer, a vintner, a carter, a butcher, and a baker. You will give me their descriptions, your Excellency?"

Herbeck read the postscript.

"But you don't tell him who - "

"Why should he know?" said Herbeck, glancing shrewdly at the duke. "His ignorance will be all the better for the plot."

"Then this is big game, your Highness?" asked the chief.

"Big game."

"One is as big and powerful as a Carpathian bear. Look out," warned Herbeck.

"And he is?"

"The mountaineer."

"And the vintner?"

"Oh, he is a little fellow, and hasn't grown his bite yet," said Herbeck dryly.

The duke laughed again. It would be as good as a play.

"I thank you, Herbeck. You have neatly arranged a fine comedy. I do not think so clearly as I used to. When the arrest is made, give it as much publicity as possible. Take a squad of soldiers; it will give it a military look. Will you be on the field this afternoon?"

"No, your highness," touching the papers which strewed his desk; "this will keep me busy well into evening."

The duke waved his hand cheerfully and left the cabinet.

"Your excellency, then, really leaves me to work in the dark?" asked the chief uneasily.

"Yes," tearing up the note. "But you will not be in the dark long after you have arrested these persons. Begin with the mountaineer and the vintner; the others do not matter so much." Then Herbeck laughed. The chief raised his head. He had not heard his excellency laugh like that in many moons. "Report to me your progress. Unfortunately my informant does not state just where these fellows are to be found."

"That is my business, your Excellency."

"Good luck to you!" responded Herbeck, with a gesture of dismissal.

When her highness came in from her morning's ride she found the duke waiting in her apartments.

"Why, father," kissing him, "what brings you here?"

"A little idea I have in mind." He drew her down to the arm of the chair. "We all have our little day-dreams."

"Who does not, father?" She slid her arm round his neck. She was full of affection for this kindly parent.

"But there are those of us who must not accept day-dreams as realities; for then there will be heartaches and futile longings."

"You are warning me. About what, father?" There was a little stab in her heart.

"Herr Carmichael is a fine fellow, brave, witty, shrewd. If all Americans are like him, America will soon become a force in the world. I have taken a fancy to him; and you know what they say of your father - no formality with those whom he likes. Humanly, I am right; but in the virtue of everyday events in court life, I am wrong."

She moved uneasily.

He went on: "Herbeck has spoken of it, the older women speak of it; and they all say - "

"Say!" she cried hotly, leaping to her feet. "What do I care what they say? Are you not the grand duke, and am I not your daughter?"

In his turn the duke felt the stab.

"You must ride no more with Herr Carmichael. It is neither wise nor safe."

"Father!"

He was up, with his arms folding round her. "Child, it is only for your sake. Listen to me. I married your mother because I loved her and she loved me. The case is isolated, rare, out of the beaten path in the affairs of rulers. But you, you must be a princess. You must steel your heart against the invasion of love, unless it comes from a state equal or superior to your own. It is harsh and cruel, but it is a law that will neither bend nor break. Do you understand me?"

The girl stared blindly at the wall. "Yes, father."

"It is all my fault," said the duke, deeply agitated, for the girl trembled under his touch.

"I shall not ride with him any more."

"There's a good girl," patting her shoulder.

"I have been a princess such a little while."

He kissed the wheaten-colored hair. "Be a brave heart, and I shall engage to find a king for you."

"I don't want any playthings, father," with the old light touch; and then she looked him full in the eyes. "I promise to do nothing more to create comment if, on the other hand, you will promise to give me two years more of freedom."

The duke readily assented, and shortly returned to his own

suite, rather pleased that there had been no scene; not that he had expected any.

Now that she was alone, she slipped into the chair, beat a light tattoo with her riding-whip against her teeth, and looked fixedly at the wall again, as if to gaze beyond it, into the dim future. But she saw nothing save that she was young and that the days in Dresden, for all their penury, were far pleasanter than these.

Meantime the chief of police called his subaltern and placed in his hands the peculiar descriptions. The word vintner caused him to give vent to an ejaculation of surprise.

"He was in here last night. I have had him followed all day. He lives over the American consulate. Among his things was found the uniform of a colonel in the Prussian Uhlans."

"Ha! Arrest him to-morrow, or the day after at the latest. But the mountaineer is the big game. Do not arrest the vintner till you have him. Where one is the other is likely to be. But on the moment of arrest you must have a squad of soldiers at your back."

"Soldiers?" doubtfully.

"Express orders of his highness."

"It shall be done."

Considerable activity was manifest in the police bureau the rest of that day.

To return to Carmichael. He had never before concerned himself with resignations. Up to this hour he had never resigned anything he had set his heart upon. So it was not an easy matter for him to compose a letter to the secretary of state, resigning the post at Dreiberg. True, he added that he desired to be transferred to a seaport town, France or Italy preferred. The high altitude in Dreiberg had affected his heart. However, in case there was no other available post, they would kindly appoint his successor at once. Carmichael never faltered where his courage was concerned, and it needed a fine quality of moral courage to write this letter and enclose it in the diplomatic pouch which went into the mails that night. It took courage indeed to face the matter squarely and resolutely, when there was the urging desire to linger on and on, indefinitely. That she was not going to marry the king of Jugendheit did not alter his affairs in the least. It was all hopeless, absurd, and impossible. He must go.

Some one was knocking on the door.

"Come in."

"A letter for your excellency," said the concierge.

"Wait till I read it. There may be an answer."

"If Herr Carmichael would learn the secret of number forty Krumerweg, let him attire himself as a vintner and be in the Krumerweg at eight o'clock to-night."

This note was as welcome to the recipient as the flowers in the spring. An adventure? He was ready, now and always. Anything to take his mind off his own dismal affairs. Then he recalled the woman in black; the letter could apply to none but her. More than this, he might light upon the puzzle regarding the vintner. He had met the fellow before. But where?

"What sort of clothes does a vintner wear?" he asked.

"A vintner, your Excellency?"

"Yes. I shall need the costume of a vintner this evening."

"Oh, that will be easy," affirmed the concierge, "if your excellency does not mind wearing clothes that have already been worn."

"My excellency will not care a hang. Procure them as soon as you can."

So it came about that Carmichael, dressed as a vintner, his hat over his eyes, stole into the misty night and took the way to the Krumerweg. He knew exactly where he wished to go: number forty. It was gray-black in the small streets; and but for the occasional light in a window the dark would have had no modification. Sometimes he would lose the point of the compass and blunder against a wall or find himself feeling for the curb, hesitant of foot. The wayside shrine was a rift in the gloom, and he knew that he had only a few more steps to take. After all, who was the lady in black and why should he bother himself about her? She probably came from the back stairs of the palace. And yet, the chancellor himself had been in this place. What should he do? Should he wait across the street? Should he knock at the door and ask to be admitted? No; he must skulk in the dark, on the opposite side. He picked his way over the street and stood for a moment in the denser black.

A step? He trained his ear. But even as he did so his arms were grasped firmly and twisted behind his back, and at the same time a cloth was wrapped round the lower part of his face, leaving only his eyes and nose visible. It was all so sudden and unexpected that he was passive the first few seconds; after that there was some scuffling, strenuous, too. He was fighting against three. Desperately he surged this

Harold MacGrath

way and that. Even in the heat of battle he wondered a little why no one struck him; they simply clung to him, and at length he could not move. His hands were tied, not roughly, but surely. In all this commotion, not a whisper, not a voice; only heavy breathing.

Then one of the three whistled. A minute or two after a closed carriage came into the Krumerweg, and Carmichael was literally bundled inside. His feet were now bound. Two of his captors sat on the forward seat, while the third joined the driver. Carmichael could distinguish nothing but outlines and shadows. He choked, for he was furious. To be trussed like this, without any explanation whatever! What the devil was going on? Unanswered.

The carriage began to move slowly. It had to; swift driving in the Krumerweg was hardly possible and at no time safe. Carmichael set himself to note the turns of the street. One turn after another he counted, fixing as well as he could the topography of the town through which they were passing. At last he realized that they were leaving Dreiberg behind and were going down the mountain on the north side, toward Jugendheit. Once the level road was reached, a fast pace was set and maintained for miles. At the Ehrenstein barrier no question was asked, and Carmichael's one hope was shattered. At the Jugendheit barrier the carriage stopped. There were voices. Carmichael saw the flicker of a lantern. His captors got out. Presently there appeared at the door an old man dressed as a mountaineer. In his hand was the lantern.

"Pardon me, dear nephew - Fools!" he broke off, swinging round. "He has tricked you all. This is not *he*!"

Three astonished faces peered over the old man's shoulder. Carmichael eyed them evilly. He now saw that one was a carter, another a butcher, and the third a baker. He had seen them before, in the Black Eagle. But this signified nothing.

"Untie him and take off that rag. It may be Scharfenstein." The old man possessed authority.

Carmichael, freed, stretched himself.

"Well?" he said, with a dangerous quiet.

"Herr Carmichael, the American consul!" The old man nearly dropped the lantern. "Oh, you infernal blockheads!"

"Explanations are in order," suggested Carmichael.

"You are offered a thousand apologies for a stupid mistake. Now, may I ask how you came to be dressed in these clothes on this particular night?"

Carmichael's anger dissolved, and he laughed. All the mystery was gone with the abruptness of a mist under the first glare of the sun. He saw how neatly he had been duped. He still carried the note. This he gave to the leader of this midnight expedition.

"Humph!" said the old man in a growl. "I thought as much." He whispered to his companions. "Herr Carmichael, I shall have the honor of escorting you back to Dreiberg."

"But will it be as easy to go in as it was to come out?"

"Trust you for that. The American consul's word will be sufficient for our needs."

"And if I refuse to give that word?"

"In that case, you will have to use your legs," curtly.

"I prefer to ride."

"Thanks. I shall sit with the driver."

"That also will please me."

"And you ask no further questions?"

"Why should I? I know all I wish to know, which is more than you would care to have me."

The mountaineer swore.

"If we talk any longer I shall be late for breakfast."

"Forward, then!"

On the way, it all came back to Carmichael with the vividness of a forgotten photograph, come upon suddenly: Bonn, the Rhine, swift and turbulent, a tow-headed young fellow who could not swim well, his own plunge, his fingers in the flaxen hair, and the hard fight to the landing; all this was a tale twice told.

Vintner? Not much!

CHAPTER XVI

HER FAN

It was dawn when they began to pull up the road to Dreiberg. The return had been leisurely despite Carmichael's impatience. In the military field the troops were breaking camp for their departure to the various posts throughout the duchy. Only the officers, who were to attend the court ball that evening, and the resident troops would remain. The maneuvers were over; the pomp of miniature war was done. Carmichael peered through the window. What a play yonder scene was to what he had been through! To break camp before dawn, before breakfast, rain and hail and snow smothering one; when the frost-bound iron of the musket caught one's fingers and tore the skin; the shriek of shot overhead, the boom of cannon and the gulp of impact; cold, hungry, footsore, sleepy; here and there a comrade crumpling up strangely and lying still and white; the muddy ruts in the road; the whole world a dead gray like the face of death! What did those yonder know of war?

The carriage stopped.

"I shall not intrude, I trust?" said the old man, opening the door and getting in.

Harold MacGrath

"Not now," replied Carmichael. "What is all this about?"

"A trifle; I might say a damn-fool trifle. But what did you mean when you said you knew all you wanted to know?" The mountaineer showed some anxiety.

"Exactly what I said. The only thing that confuses me is the motive."

The old man thought for a while. "Suppose you had a son who was making a fool of himself?"

"Or a nephew?"

"Well, or a nephew?"

"Making a fool of himself over what?"

"A woman."

"Nothing unusual in that. But what kind of a woman?"

"A good woman, honest, too good by far for any man."

"Oh!"

"Suppose she was vastly his inferior in station, that marriage to him was merely a political contract? What would you do?"

"I believe I begin to understand."

"I am grateful for that."

"But the risks you run!"

"I believed them all over last night."

"But you would dare handle him in this way?"

"When the devil drives, my friend!" The other smiled. "I was born in the heart of a war. I have taken so many risks that the sense of danger no longer has a keen edge. But now that you understand, I am sure a soldier like yourself will pardon the blunder of last night."

"Your nephew is an ungrateful wretch."

"What?" coldly.

"He knew all along who I was. I dragged him out of the Rhine upon a certain day, and he plays this trick!"

"You? Carmichael, Carmichael; of course; I should have remembered the name, as he wrote me at the time. Thank you! And you knew him all the while?"

"No; I recalled his face, but the time and place were in the dark till this early morning. Here we are at the gates. What's this? Guards? I never saw them at these gates before."

"You will make yourself known to them?"

"Yes. But if they question me?"

"Wink. Every soldier knows what that means."

"When a fellow turns in early in the morning?" Carmichael laughed hilariously.

"I ask you frankly not to let them question me. When I left the city last night I never expected to return."

"I'll do what I can."

Carmichael bared his head and leaned out of the window. He recognized one of the guards. A policeman in military uniform!

"Good morning!" said Carmichael.

"Herr Carmichael?" surprised. "Your excellency?"

"Yes. I've been having a little junket, I and my friend here." And Carmichael winked.

"Ah!"

"But what - "

"Sh! Very important affair," said the disguised officer. "Go on."

But after the carriage had passed it occurred to him that Carmichael wore a dress like a vintner's and that his friend was a mountaineer! *Du lieber Himmel!* What kind of a mix-up was this? The chancellor never could have meant Carmichael!

"Thanks!" whispered the old man.

"Did you see the soldier?"

"Yes."

"He is one of the police in disguise. Be on your guard. If you don't mind I'll use this carriage to the hotel."

"You are a thousand times welcome. I will leave you here. And take the advice of an old man who has seen the four sides of humanity: leave falling in love to poets and to fools!"

The mountaineer got out quickly, closed the door, spoke a word to the driver, and slipped into an alleyway.

Carmichael arrived at the Grand Hotel in time to see her serene highness, accompanied by two of her ladies and an escort of four soldiers, start out for her morning ride. The zest of his own strange adventure died. He waited till they had passed, then slunk into the hotel. The concierge gazed at him in amazement. Carmichael winked. The concierge smiled. He understood. *Americaner* or *Ehrensteiner*, the young fellows were all the same.

"Police at the gates," mused Carmichael, as he soaked his head and face in cold water. "By George, it looks as if my friend the vintner was in for some excitement! Far be it that I should warn him. He had his little joke; I can wait for mine."

Gretchen! Carmichael stopped, his collar but half-way around his throat. Gretchen, brave, kindly, beautiful Gretchen! Now, by the Lord, that should not be! He would wring the vintner's neck. He snapped the collar viciously. He was not in an amiable mood this fair September morning. And when some one hammered on the door he called sharply.

Grumbach entered.

"You are angry about something," he said.

"So I am, but you are always welcome."

"You have overslept?"

"No; on the contrary."

"Poker?"

"After a fashion," said Carmichael, the grumble gone from his voice. "I was beaten by three of a kind."

"So?"

"But I found a good hand later."

"Kings."

"Four?"

"Oh, no; only one. I haven't drawn yet."

"You are not telling me all."

"No. You are going to the ball to-night?"

"I would not miss it for five thousand crowns," sadly.

"You look as if you were going to a funeral instead of the greatest event of the year in Dreiberg."

"I didn't sleep well either."

"Out?"

"No; one does not have to go out in order not to sleep."

"I'd like to know what's going on in that bullet-head of yours."

"Nothing is going on; everything has stopped."

"Can't you make a confidant of me, Hans?"

"Not yet, Captain."

"When you are ready it may be too late. I leave Dreiberg for good in a few weeks."

"No!" For the first time Grumbach showed interest.

"I have resigned the consulship."

"And for what reason?"

Carmichael silently drew on his coat.

"Ach! So you have one, too?"

"One what?"

"One secret."

"Yes. But it's the kind we can't talk about."

"I understand. Have you had breakfast?"

"Neither have I. Let us go together. It may be we need each other's company this morning. You and I won't have to bother about talking."

"You make a good comrade, Hans."

* * * * *

There was a large crowd outside the palace that night, which was clear and starry. A troop of cavalry patrolled the fence. Carriage after carriage rolled in through the gates, coming directly from the opera. It was eleven o'clock. All the great in the duchy were on hand that night. Often a cheer rose from the ranks of the outsiders as some popular general or some famous beauty passed. It was an orderly crowd, jostling and

Harold MacGrath

good-natured, held only by curiosity. Every window in the palace presented a glowing square of light; and beams crisscrossed the emerald lawns and died in the arms of the lurking shadows. The gardens were illuminated besides. It was fairy-land, paid for by those who were not entitled to enter. Few, however, thought of this inconsistency. A duchy is a duchy; nothing more need be said.

Carmichael was naturally democratic. To ride a block in a carriage was to him a waste of time. And he rather liked to shoulder into a press. With the aid of his cane and a frequent push of the elbow he worked his way to the gates. And close by the sentry-box he saw Gretchen and her vintner. Carmichael could not resist stopping a moment. He raised his hat to Gretchen, to the wonder of those nearest. The vintner would have gladly disappeared, but the human wall behind made this impossible. But he was needlessly alarmed. Carmichael only smiled ironically.

"Do you know where the American consulate is?" he asked low, so that none but Gretchen and the vintner heard.

"Yes," said the vintner, blushing with shame.

"I live above the agency."

"Good! I shall expect to see you in the morning."

But the vintner was determined that he shouldn't. He would be at work in the royal vineyards on the morrow.

"To-morrow?" repeated Gretchen, to whom this by-play was a blank. "Why should he wish to see you?"

"Who knows? Let us be going. They are pressing us too close to the gates."

"Very well," acquiesced Gretchen, somewhat disappointed. She wanted to see all there was to be seen.

"It is half-after ten," he added, as if to put forward some logical excuse for leaving at this moment.

A man followed them all the way to the Krumerweg.

Carmichael threw himself eagerly into the gaiety of the dance. Never had he seen the ball-room so brilliant with color. Among all those there his was the one somber dress. The white cambric stock and the frill in his shirt were the only gay touches. It was not his fault: the rules of the service compelled him thus to dress. But he needed no brass or cloth of gold. There was not a male head among all the others to compare with his.

He was an accomplished waltzer, after the manner of that day, when one went round and round like some mechanical toy wound up. Strauss and Waldteufel tingled his feet; and he whirled ambassadors' wives till they were breathless and ambassadors' daughters till they no longer knew or cared where they were. He was full of subtle deviltry this night, with an undercurrent of malice toward every one and himself in particular. This would be the last affair of the kind for him, and he wanted a full memory of it. Between times he exchanged a jest or two with the chancellor or talked battles with old Ducwitz; twice he caught the grand duke's eye, but there was only a friendly nod from that august personage, no invitation to talk. Thrice, while on the floor, her highness passed him; but there was never a smile, never a glance. He became careless and reckless. He would seek her and talk to her and smile at her even if the duke threw a regiment in between. The Irish blood in him burned to-night, capable of any folly. He no longer danced. He waited and watched; and it was during one of these waits that he saw Grumbach in the gallery.

"Now, what the devil is the Dutchman doing with a pair of opera-glasses!"

It required some time and patience to discover the object of this singular attention on the part of Grumbach. Carmichael was finally convinced that this object was no less a person than her serene highness!

Later her highness stood before one of the long windows in the conservatory, listlessly watching the people in the square. And these poor fools envied her! To envy her, who was a prisoner, a chattel to be exchanged for war's immunity, who was a princess in name but a cipher in fact! All was wrong with the world. She had stolen out of the ball-room; the craving to be alone had been too strong. Little she cared whether they missed her or not. She left the window and sat on one of the divans, idly opening and shutting her fan. Was that some one coming for her? She turned.

It was Carmichael.

What an opportunity for scandal! She laughed inwardly. The barons and their wives, the ambassadors' wives and their daughters, would miss them both. And the spirit of deviltry lay also upon her heart. She smiled at the man and with her fan bade him be seated at her side. The divinity that hedges in a king did not bother either of them just then.

"You have not asked me to dance to-night," she declared.

"I know it."

"Why?"

"I am neither a prince nor an ambassador."

"But you *have* danced with me."

"Yes; I have been to Heaven now and then."

"And do you eject yourself thus easily?"

"By turning myself out my self-esteem remains unruffled."

"Then you expected to be turned out?"

"Sooner or later."

"Why?"

Again that word! To him it was the most tantalizing word in the language. It crucified him.

"Why?" she repeated, her eyes soft and dreamy.

"As I have said, I am not a prince. I am only a consul, not even a diplomat, simply a business arm of my government. My diplomacy never ascends above the quality of hops and wines imported. I am supposed to take in any wandering sailor, feed him, and ship him home. I am also the official guide of all American tourists."

"That is no reason."

"Your father - " He should have said the grand duke.

"Ah, yes; my father, the chancellor, the ambassadors, and their wives and daughters! I begin to believe that you have grown afraid of them."

"I confess that I have. I had an adventure last night. Would you like to hear about it?"

How beautiful she was in that simple gown of white, unadorned by any jewels save the little crown of sparkling white stones in her hair!

"Tell me."

He was a good story-teller. It was a crisp narrative he made.

"A veiled lady," she mused. "What would you say if I told you that your mystery is no mystery at all? I am the veiled lady. And the person I went to see was my old nurse, my foster-mother, with whom I spent the happiest, freest days of my life, in the garret at Dresden. Pouf! All mysteries may be dispelled if we go to the right person. So you are to be recalled?"

"I have asked for my recall, your Highness."

"And so Dreiberg no longer appeals to you? You once told inc that you loved it."

"I am cursed with *wanderlust*, your Highness." He regretted that he had not remained in the ball-room. He was in great danger.

"You promised to tell me what she is like." Suddenly all his fear went away, all his trepidation; the spirit of recklessness which had vised him a little while ago again empowered him. He was afraid of nothing. His face flushed and there were bright points of fire in his eyes. She saw what she had roused, and grew afraid herself. She pretended to become interested in the Watteau cupids on her fan.

"How shall I describe her?" he said. "I have seen only paintings and marbles, and these are inanimate. I have never seen angels, so I can not draw a comparison there. Have you ever seen ripe wheat in a rain-storm? That is the color of her hair. There is jade and lapis-lazuli in her eyes. And Ole Bull could not imitate the music of her voice." He leaned toward her. "And I love her better than life, better than hope; and between us there is the distance of a thousand worlds. So I must give up the dream and go away, as an honorable man should."

Neither of them heard the chancellor's approach.

"And because I love her."

The fan in her hand slipped unheeded to the floor.

"Your Highness," broke in the cold even tones of Herbeck, "your father is making inquiries about you."

Carmichael rose instantly, white as the frill in his shirt.

Hildegarde, however, was a princess. She gained her feet leisurely, with half a smile on her lips.

"Count, Herr Carmichael tells me that he is soon to leave Dreiberg."

"Ah!" There was satisfaction in Herbeck's ejaculation, satisfaction of a frank order. But there was a glint of admiration in his eyes as he recognized the challenge in Carmichael's. He saw that he must step carefully in regard to this hot-headed young Irishman. "We shall miss Herr Carmichael."

Her highness moved serenely toward the door. Carmichael

waited till she was gone from sight, then he stooped and picked up the fan. Herbeck at once held out his hand.

"Give it to me, Herr Captain," he said, with a melancholy gentleness. "I will return it to her highness."

Carmichael deliberately thrust the fan into a pocket and shook his head.

"Your Excellency, I do not know how long you stood behind us, but you were there long enough to learn that I have surrendered my dream. Nothing but force will cause me to surrender this fan."

"Keep it, then, my son," replied the chancellor, with good understanding.

CHAPTER XVII

AFTER THE VINTAGE

The ducal vineyards covered some forty acres of rich hillside. All day long the sun beat squarely upon the clustering fruit. A low rambling building of stone covered the presses and bottling departments, and was within comparatively easy distance of the city. During the vintage several hundred men and women found employment. The grand duke derived a comfortable private revenue from these wines, the Tokay being scarcely inferior to that made in Hungary. There was a large brewery besides, which supplied all the near-by cities and towns. The German noble, be he king, duke, or baron, has always been more or less a merchant; and it did not embarrass the grand duke of Ehrenstein in the least to see his coat of arms burnt into oaken wine-casks.

A former steward had full charge of the business, personally hiring and paying the help and supervising the various branches. He was a gruff old fellow, just and honest; and once you entered his employ he was as much a martinet as any captain at sea. The low cunning of the peasant never eluded his watchful eye. He knew to the last pound of grapes how much wine there should be, how much beer to the last measure of hops.

Harold MacGrath

The entrance to the vineyards was made through a small lodge where the ducal vintner lived, and kept his books and moneys till such time as he should be required to place them before the proper official.

Upon this brave morning, the one following the ball at the palace, the vintner was reclining against the outside wall of the gates, smoking his china-pipe and generally at peace with the world. The bloom was early upon the grape, work was begun, and the vintage promised to be exceptionally fine. Through a drifting cloud of smoke he discerned a solitary figure approaching from the direction of Dreiberg, a youthful figure, buoyant of step, and confident. Herr Hoffman was rather interested. Ordinarily the peasant who came to this gate had his hat in his hand and his feet were laggard. Not so this youth. He paused at the gate and inspected the old man highly.

"Herr Hoffman?"

"Yes."

"I want work."

"So? What can you do?" He was a clean youngster, this, but there was something in his eyes that vaguely disturbed the head vintner. It was like mockery more than anything else. The youth recounted his abilities, and Hoffman was gracious enough to admit that he seemed to know what he was talking about.

"I have a letter to you also."

"*Ach!* We shall be properly introduced now," said Hoffman, growling. "Let me see it."

He saw it, but with starting eyes. There was, then, something new under the sun? A picker of grapes, recommended by a princess! He turned the letter inside out, but found no illumination.

"*Du lieber Gott!* You are Leopold Dietrich?"

"Yes, Herr."

"How did you come by this letter?"

"Her serene highness is patron to Gretchen, the goose-girl, at whose request the recommendation was given me."

This altered matters. "Follow me," said Hoffman.

The two entered the office.

"Can you write?"

"A little, Herr."

"Then write your name on this piece of paper and that. Each night you will present yours with the number of pounds, which will be credited to you. You must bring it back each morning. If you lose it you will be paid nothing for your labor."

Dietrich wrote his name twice. It was rather hard work, for he screwed up his mouth and cramped his fingers. Still, Hoffman was not wholly satisfied with his eyes.

"Gottlieb," he said to one of the men, "take him to terrace ninety-eight. That hasn't been touched yet. We'll see what sort of workman he is." He spoke to Dietrich again. "What is Gretchen to you?" For Hoffman knew Gretchen; many a time she had filled her basket and drawn her crowns.

"She is my sweetheart, Herr." And there was no mockery in the youth's eyes as he said this.

"Take him along, Gottlieb. You will have no further use for this letter from her highness, so I'll keep it and frame it and hang it in the office." Which showed that Hoffman himself had had lessons in the gentle art of mockery.

Terrace ninety-eight was given over to small grapes; thus, many bunches had to be picked to fill the basket. But Dietrich went to work with a will. His fingers were deft and his knife was sharp; and by midsun he had turned his sixth basket, which was fair work, considering.

As Hoffman did not feed his employees, Dietrich was obliged to beg from his co-workers. Very willingly they shared with him their coarse bread and onions. He ate the bread and stuffed the onions in his pocket. There was no idling. As soon as the frugal meal was over, the peasants trooped away to their respective terraces. Once more the youth was alone. He set down his basket and laughed. Was there ever such a fine world? Had there ever been a more likable adventure? The very danger of it was the spice which gave it flavor. He stretched out his arms as if to embrace this world which appeared so rosal, so joyous to his imagination.

"Thanks, thanks! You have given me youth, and I accept it," he said aloud, perhaps addressing that mutable goddess who presides over all follies. "Regret it in my old age? Not I! I shall have lived for one short month. Youth was given to us to enjoy, and I propose to press the grape to the final drop. And when I grow old this adventure shall be the tonic to wipe out many wrinkles of care. A mad fling, a brimming cup, one short merry month - and then, the reckoning! How I hate the thought!"

He sobered; the laughter went out of his eyes and face. Changeful twenty, where so many paths reach out into the great world, paths straight and narrow, of devious turnings which end at precipices, of blind alleys which lead nowhere and close in behind!

"I love her, I love her!" His face grew bright again, and the wooing blood ran tingling in his veins. "Am I a thief, a scoundrelly thief, because I have that right common to all men, to love one woman? Some day I shall suffer for this; some day my heart shall ache; so be it!"

The sun began the downward circle; the shadows crept eastward and imperceptibly grew longer; a gray tone settled under the stones at his feet. Sometimes he sang, sometimes he stood dreaming. His fingers were growing sore and sticky and there was a twinge in his back as he shouldered his eighth basket and scrambled down to the man who weighed the pick. He was beginning his ninth when he saw Gretchen coming along the purple aisle. She waved a hand in welcome, and he sheathed his knife. No more work this day for him. He waited.

"What a beautiful day!" said Gretchen, with a happy laugh.

"Aye, what a day for love!"

"And work!"

"Kiss me!"

"When you fill that basket."

"Not before?"

Harold MacGrath

"Not even a little one," mischief in her glance. Out came the knife and the vintner plied himself furiously. Gretchen had a knife of her own, and she joined him. They laughed gaily. Snip, snip; bunch by bunch the contents of the basket grew.

"There!" he said at last. "That's what I call work; but it is worth it. Now!"

Gretchen saw that it would be futile to hold him off longer; what she would not give he would of a surety take. So she put her hands behind her back, closed her eyes, and raised her chin. He kissed not only the lovely mouth, but the eyes and cheeks and hair.

"Gretchen, you are as good and beautiful as an angel."

"What are angels like?"

"An angel is the most beautiful woman a poet can describe or imagine."

"Then there are no men angels?"

"Only Gabriel; at least I never heard of any other."

"Then I do not want to be an angel. I had rather be what I am. Besides, angels do not have tempers; they do not long for things they should not have; they have no sweethearts." She caught him roughly by the arms. "Ah, if anything should happen to you, I should die! It seems as though I had a hundred hearts and that they had all melted into one for love of you. Do men love as women love? Is it everything and all things, or only an incident? I would give up my soul to you if you asked for it."

"I ask only for your love, Gretchen; only that." And he pressed her hands. "All men are rogues, more or less. There are so many currents and eddies entering into a man's life. It is made up of a thousand variant interests. No, man's love is never like a woman's. But remember this, Gretchen, I loved you the best I knew how, as a man loves but once, honorably as it was possible, purely and dearly."

The shade of trouble crossed her face. "Why are you always talking like that? Do I not know that you love me? Have I not my dowry, and are we not to be married after the vintage?"

"But your singing?"

"Singing? Why, my voice belongs to you; for your sake I wish to be great, for no other reason."

He ripped a bunch of grapes from the vine, a thing no careful vintner should do, and held it toward her.

"Have you ever heard of the kissing cherries?" he asked.

She shook her head. He explained.

"This bunch will do very well."

He took one grape at the bottom in his teeth. Gingerly Gretchen did the same. Their lips met in a smothered laughter. Then they tried it again.

And this Watteau picture met the gaze of two persons on the terrace below. The empurpling face of one threatened an explosion, but the smiling face of the other restrained this vocal thunder. The old head vintner kicked a stone savagely, and at this rattling noise Gretchen and her lover turned. They beheld the steward, and peering over his shoulder the amused countenance of the Princess Hildegarde.

"You - " began the steward, no longer able to contain himself.

"Patience, Hoffman!" warned her highness. Then she laughed blithely. It was such a charming picture, and never had she seen a handsomer pair of bucolic lovers. A sudden pang drove the merriment from her face. Ah, but she envied Gretchen! For the peasant there was freedom, there was the chosen mate; but for the princess -

"Your hat, scoundrel!" cried Hoffman.

The vintner snatched off his hat apologetically and swung it round on the tips of his fingers.

"Is this the way you work?"

"I have picked nine baskets."

"You should have picked twelve."

It interested her highness to note that this handsome young fellow was not afraid of the head vintner. So this was Gretchen's lover? He was really handsome; there was nothing coarse about his features or figure. And presently she realized that he was returning her scrutiny with interest. He had never seen her highness at close range before, and he now saw that Gretchen was more beautiful only because he saw her through the eyes of a lover.

The pause was broken by Gretchen.

"Pardon, Highness!"

"For what, Gretchen?"

"For not having seen your approach."

"That was my fault, not yours. When is the wedding?"

"After the vintage, Highness."

Her highness then spoke to the bridegroom-elect. "You will be good to her?"

"Who could help it, your Highness?"

The pronoun struck her oddly, for peasants as a usual thing never used it in addressing the nobility.

"Well, on the day of the wedding I will stand sponsor to you both. And good luck go with you. Come, Hoffman; my horse will be restive and my men impatient."

She passed down the aisle, and the head vintner followed, wagging his head. He was not at all satisfied with that tableau. He employed men to work; he wanted no love-affairs inside his vineyards. As for her highness, she had come for the sole purpose of seeing Gretchen's lover; and it occurred to her that the really desirable men were generally unencumbered by titles.

"He will discharge me," said the young vintner gloomily.

"He will not dare," returned Gretchen. "We have done nothing wrong. Her highness will stand by us. It must be five o'clock," looking at the sun.

"In that case, no more work for the day."

He swung the basket to his shoulder, and the sun, flashing upon its contents, turned the bloomy globes into dull rubies. He presented his card at the office and was duly credited with three crowns, which, according to Gretchen, was a fine day's work. Hoffman said nothing about dismissal.

"Come day after to-morrow; to-morrow is a feast-day. You are always having feast-days when work begins. All summer long you loaf about, but the minute you start to work you must find excuses to lay off. Clear out, both of you!"

"Work at last," said Dietrich, as he and Gretchen started for the city. "If I can get a position in the brewery for the winter I shall be rich."

"Oh, the beautiful world!"

"Do you recall the first day I met you?" he asked.

"Yes. A little more and that dog would have killed the big gander. What little things bring about big ones! When I walked into the city that day, had any one told me that I should fall in love, I should have laughed."

"And I!"

Arm in arm they went on. Sometimes Gretchen sang; often he put her hand to his lips. By and by they came abreast of an old Gipsy. He wore a coat of Joseph's, and his face was as lined as a frost-bitten apple. But his eyes were keen and undimmed, and he walked confidently and erect, like a man who has always lived in the open.

"Will you tell me how to find the Adlergasse?" he asked in broken German. His accent was that of a Magyar. He had a smattering of a dozen tongues at his command, for in his time he had crossed and recrossed the Danube, the Rhine, and the Rhone.

They carelessly gave him specific directions and passed on. He followed grimly, like fate, whose agent he was, though long delayed. When he reached the Adlergasse he looked for a sign. He came to a stop in front of the dingy shop of the clock-mender. He went inside, and the ancient clock-mender looked up from his work, for he was always working.

He rose wearily and asked what he could do for his customer. His eyes were bothering him, so the fact that the man was a Gipsy did not at first impress him.

The Gipsy smiled mysteriously and laid a hand on his heart.

"Who are you?" sharply demanded the clock-mender.

"Who I am does not matter. I am he whom you seek."

"God in Heaven!" The bony hands of the clock-mender shot out and clutched the other's coat in a grip which shook, so intense was it. The Gipsy released himself slowly. "But first show me your pretty crowns and the paper which will give me immunity from the police. I know something about you. You never break your word. That is why I came. Your crowns, as you offered, and immunity; then I speak."

"Man, I can give you the crowns, but God knows I have no longer the power to give you immunity."

"So?"

The Gipsy shouldered his bundle.

"For God's sake, wait!" begged the clock-mender.

But the Gipsy walked out, unheeding.

CHAPTER XVIII

A WHITE SCAR

Two days later, in the afternoon.

"Grumbach," said Carmichael, "what the deuce were you looking at the other night, with those opera-glasses?"

"At the ball?" Grumbach pressed down the ash in his pipe and brushed his thumb on his sleeve. "I was looking into the past."

"With a pair of opera-glasses?"

"Yes." Grumbach was perfectly serious.

"Oh, pshaw! You were following her highness with them. I want to know why."

"She is beautiful."

"You made a promise to me not long ago."

"I did?" non-committally.

"Yes. Soon I shall be shaking the dust of Dreiberg, and I

want to know beforehand what this Chinese puzzle is. What did you do that compelled your flight from Ehrenstein?"

Grumbach's pipe hung pendulent in his hand. He swung it to and fro absently.

"I am waiting. Remember, you are an American citizen, for all that you were born here. If anything should happen to you, I must know the whole story in order to help you. You know that you may trust me."

"It isn't that, Captain. I have grown to like you in these few days."

"What has that to do with it?" impatiently.

"Nothing, perhaps. Only, if I tell you, you will not be my friend."

"Nonsense! What you did sixteen years ago doesn't matter now. It is enough for me that you fought in my regiment, and that you were a brave soldier."

"Those opera-glasses; it was an idea. Well, since you will know. I was a gardener's boy. I worked under my brother Hermann. I used to ask the nurse, who had charge of her serene highness, where she would go each day. Then I'd cut flowers and meet them on the road somewhere and give the bouquet to the child. There was never any escort; a footman and a driver. The little one was always greatly pleased, and she would call me Hans. I was in love those days." Grumbach laughed with bitterness. "Yes, even I. Her name was Tekla, and she was a jade. I wanted to run away, but I had no money. I had already secured a passport; no matter how. It was the first affair, and I was desperately hurt. One day a Gipsy came to me. I shall always know him by the yellow spot in one of his black eyes. I was given a thousand crowns to tell him which road her highness was to be driven over the next day. As I said, I was mad with love. Why a Gipsy should want to know where her highness was going to ride was of no consequence to me. I told him. I was to get the money the same night. It was thus that her highness was stolen; it was thus that I became accessory before the fact, as the lawyers say. Flight with a band of Magyar Gipsies; weary days in the mountains, with detachments of troops scouring the whole duchy. Finally I escaped. A fortune was offered for the immediate return of the child. At the time I believed that it was an abduction for ransom. But no one ever came forward for the reward. There was a price on my head when it was known that I had fled." Grumbach stared into his pipe without seeing anything.

"And no one ever came for the reward? That is strange. Was immunity promised?" asked Carmichael.

"It was inferred, but not literally promised."

"Fear kept them away."

"Perhaps. And there is Arnsberg."

"Was he guilty?"

"I never saw *his* hand anywhere."

"So this is the story! Well, when a man's in love he is, more or less, in the clutch of temporary insanity." Carmichael's tone wasn't exactly cheery.

"Insanity! Then you do not judge me harshly?"

"No, Hans. I've a wild streak in me also. But what I can't

Harold MacGrath

understand is why you return and put your head in the lion's mouth. The police will stumble on something. I tell you frankly that if you are arrested I could do little or nothing for you. The United States protects only harmless political outcasts. Yours is a crime such as nullifies your citizenship, and any government would be compelled, according to the terms of treaty, to send you back here, if the demand was made for your extradition."

"I know all that," Grumbach replied, dumping the ash into his palm and casting it into the paper-basket.

"I suppose that when conscience drives we must go on. But the princess has been found. The best thing you can do is to put your passports into immediate use and return to the States. You can do no good here."

"Maybe." Grumbach refilled his pipe, lighted it, and without saying more went out and down into the street.

Carmichael watched him through the window. Cloud after cloud of smoke ran wavering behind the exile. He was smoking like one deeply perturbed.

"He's a queer codger, and it's a queer story. I don't believe I have heard it all, either. What was he really hunting for with those glasses? I give it up."

He was not angry with Grumbach; rather he seemed to be drawn to him more closely than ever. Mad with love. That was the phrase. He conned it over and over; mad with love. That excused many things. How strangely the chess-men were moved! Had Grumbach not assisted in the abduction, her highness would in all probability have grown up as other princesses, artificial, cold, reserved, seldom touched by the fires of animated thought or action. In fact, had things been otherwise, he never would have ridden with her highness in the freshness of the morning - or fallen in love with her. By rights he ought to curse Grumbach; but for him he would still be captain of his heart. Mad with love! There was no doubt of it. And the phrase rang in his ear for some time.

Grumbach was indeed perturbed, and this sensation was the result of what he had *not* told his friend. *Gott!* What was going on? He hadn't the least idea where his footsteps were leading him. He went on, his teeth set strongly on the horn mouthpiece of his pipe, his hands jammed in his pockets. And after a time he woke. He was in the Adlergasse. And of all that happy, noisy family, only he and Hermann left! In one of the open doorways, for it was warm, a final caress of vanishing summer, he saw a fat, youngish woman knitting woolen hose. Two or three children sprawled about her knees. There was that petulance of lip and forehead which marked the dissatisfaction of the coquette married.

"Tekla!" Grumbach murmured.

He was not conscious that he had paused, but the woman was. She eyed him with the mild indifference of the bovine. Then she dropped her glance and the shining needles clicked afresh. Grumbach forced his step onward. And for this! He laughed discordantly. The woman looked up again wonderingly. Now, why should this stranger laugh all by himself like that?

Hans saw the sign of the Black Eagle, and directed his steps thitherward. He sat down and ordered a beer, drinking it quickly. He repeated the order, but he did not touch the second glass. He threw back the lid and stared at the creamy froth as a seer stares at his ball of crystal. Carmichael was right; he was a doddering fool. What was done was done, and a thousand consciences would not right it. And what right had conscience to drag him back to Ehrenstein, where he had known the bitterest and happiest moments of his life? And yet, rail as he might at this invisible restraint called conscience, he saw God's direction in this return. Only *he*, Hans Grumbach, knew and one other. And that other, who?

Fat, Tekla was fat; and he had treasured the fair picture of her youth these long years! Well, there was an end to that. Little fat Tekla, to have nearly overturned a duchy, and never a bit the wiser! And then Hans became aware of voices close at hand, for he sat near the bar.

"Yes, Fraeu, he is at work in the grand duke's vineyards. And think, the first day he picked nine baskets."

"That is good. But I know many a one who can pick their twelve. And you are to be married when the vintage is done? You will make a fine wife, Gretchen."

"And he, a fine husband."

"And you will bring him a dowry, too. But his own people; what does he say of them?"

"He has no parents; only an uncle, who doesn't count. We shall live with grandmother and pay her rent."

"And you are wearing a new dress," admiringly.

Gretchen preened herself. Hans dropped the lid of his stein and pushed it away. His heart always warmed at the sight of this goose-girl. So she had a dowry and was going to be married? He felt of his wallet, and a kindly thought came into being. He counted down the small change for the beer, slid back his chair, and sauntered to the bar. Gretchen recognized him, and the recognition brought a smile to her face.

"Good day to you, Herr," was her greeting.

"When is the wedding?"

Gretchen blushed.

"I should like to come to it."

"You will be welcome, Herr."

"And may I bring along a little present?"

"If it so please you. I must be going," she added to Fraeu Bauer.

"May I walk along with you?" asked Hans.

"If you wish," diffidently.

So Grumbach walked with her to the Krumerweg, and he asked her many questions, and some of her answers surprised him.

"Never knew father or mother?"

"No, Herr. I am only a foundling who fell into kind hands. This is where I live."

"And if I should ask to come in?"

"But I shall be too busy to talk. This is bread-day," evasively.

"I promise to sit very quiet in a chair."

Her laughter rippled; she was always close to that expression. "You are a funny man. Come in, then; but mind, you will be dusty with flour when you leave."

"I will undertake that risk," he replied, with a seriousness not in tune with the comedy of the situation.

Into the kitchen she led him. She was moved with curiosity. Why should any man wish to see a woman knead bread?

"Sit there, Herr." And she pointed to a stool at the left of the table. The sunlight came in through the window, and an aureola appeared above her beautiful head. "Have you never seen a woman knead flour?"

"Not for many years," said Hans, thinking of his mother.

Gretchen deliberately rolled up her sleeves and began work.

There are three things which human growth never changes: the lines in the hand, the shape of the ear, and scars. The head grows, and the general features enlarge to their predestined mold, but these three things remain. Upon Gretchen's left arm, otherwise perfection, there was a white scar, rough and uneven, more like an ancient burn than anything else. Grumbach's eyes rested upon the scar and became fixed.

"Where did you get that?" he asked. He spoke with a strange calm.

"The scar? I do not remember. Grandmother says that when I was little I must have been burned."

"*Gott!*"

"What did you say, Herr?"

"Nothing. You can't remember? Think!" tensely now.

"What's all this nonsense about?" she cried, with a nervous laugh. "It's only a scar."

She went on with the kneading. She patted the dough into four squares. These she placed on the oven-stove. She wiped her hands on a cloth for that purpose, and sighed contentedly.

"There! It's a fine mystery, isn't it?"

"Yes." But Grumbach was shaking as with ague.

"What is the matter, Herr?" with concern.

"I grow dizzy like this sometimes. It doesn't amount to anything."

Gretchen turned down her sleeves. "You must go now, for I have other work."

"And so have I, Gretchen."

He gained the street, but how he never knew. He floated. Objects near at hand were shadowy and unusual. A great calm suddenly winged down upon him, and the world became clear, clear as his purpose, his courage, his duty. They might shoot or hang him, as they saw fit; this would not deter him. It might be truthfully said that he blundered back to the Grand Hotel. He must lay the whole matter before Carmichael. There lay his one hope. Carmichael should be his ambassador. But, God in Heaven, where should he begin? How?

The Gipsy, standing in the center of the walk, did not see

Grumbach, for he was looking toward the palaces, a kind of whimsical mockery in his dark eyes. Grumbach, even more oblivious, crashed into him.

Grumbach stammered an apology, and the other replied in his peculiar dialect that no harm had been done. The jar, however, had roused Hans out of his tragic musings. There was a glint of yellow in the Gipsy's eye, a flaw in the iris. Hans gave a cry.

"You? I find you at this moment, of all others?"

The Gipsy retreated. "I do not know you. It is a mistake."

"But I know you," whispered Hans. "And you will know me when I tell you that I am the gardener's boy you ruined some sixteen years ago!"

CHAPTER XIX

DISCLOSURES

The office of the American consulate in the Adlergasse ran from the front to the rear of the building. Carmichael's desk overlooked the street. But whenever a flying dream came to him he was wont to take his pipe to the chair by the rear window, whence he could view the lofty crests of the Jugendheit mountains. Directly below this window and running parallel with it was the *Biergarten* of the Black Eagle.

It is a quiet tonic to the mind to look off, to gaze at sunlit, cloud-embraced mountain peaks, Walter Pater to the contrary. Carmichael's mind that morning needed quiet, and so he came to this window; and with a smoldering pipe let himself to dreams. He was still in the uniform of the royal hunt, a meet having taken place that morning. He saw darling faces in the rugged outlines of the mountains, in the white clouds billowing across, in the patches of dazzling blue in between. Such is the fancy of a man in love!

His letter of resignation was on its way, but it would be in November before he heard definitely from the department. By that time the great snows would have blanketed the earth, and the nadir of his discontent would be reached. But what to do till that time? He could ride for some weeks, but riding without companionship was rather a lonesome affair. His own defiance of the chancellor had erected an impassable barrier between her highness and himself. They would watch him now, evade him, put small obstacles in his path, obstacles against which he could enter no reasonable complaint. A withered leaf, a glove, and a fan; these represented the sum of his romance.

Two figures moved in the garden beneath. At first he gave no attention to them. But when the two heads came together swiftly, and then separated, both smiling, he realized that he had witnessed a kiss. Ah, here was the opportunity; and, by the Lord Harry, he would not let it slip. If this fellow meant wrongly toward Gretchen - and how could he mean else? - he, Carmichael, would take the matter boldly in his hands to do some caning. He laughed. Here would be another souvenir; to have caned -

He jumped to his feet, dropped his pipe on the sill of the window, and made for his hat and sword-cane. The clerk went on with his writing. Nothing the consul did these days either alarmed or distracted him.

To gain the garden Carmichael would have to pass through the tavern. The first person he encountered was Colonel von Wallenstein. The sight of this gentleman changed his plans for the moment. He had a presentiment that this would became rather a complicated affair. He waited. Wallenstein spoke to Fraeu Bauer, who answered him with cold civility. She heartily despised this fine officer. Wallenstein twirled his mustache, laughed and went into the garden. Carmichael was in a quandary. What should he do?

Neither Gretchen nor the vintner saw Wallenstein, who remained quietly by the door. He watched them with an evil smile. He would teach this pretty fellow a lesson. After some deliberation he walked lightly toward the lovers. They did not hear him till he was almost upon them.

"A pretty picture!"

Gretchen colored and the vintner flushed, the one with dismay and the other with anger.

"A charming idyl!"

"Leave us, Gretchen," said the vintner, with a deceiving gentleness.

Gretchen started reluctantly down the path, her glance bravely before her. She knew that Wallenstein would not move; so she determined to go round him. She was not afraid to leave her vintner alone with this officer. But she miscalculated the colonel's reckless audacity. As she stepped off the path to go round him he grasped her rudely and kissed her on the cheek. She screamed as much in surprise as in anger.

And this scream brought Carmichael upon the scene. He was witness to the second kiss. He saw the vintner run forward and dash his fist into the soldier's face. Wallenstein, to whom such an assault was unexpected, fell back, hurt and blinded. The vintner, active as a cat, saw Carmichael coming on a run. He darted toward him, and before Carmichael could prevent him, dragged the sword-cane away. The blade, thin and pliant, flashed. And none too soon. The colonel had already drawn his saber.

"Save him!" Gretchen wrung her hands.

The two blades met spitefully, and there were method and

Harold MacGrath

science on both sides. But the sword-cane was no match for the broad, heavy saber. Half a dozen thrusts and parries convinced the colonel that the raging youth knew what he was doing. Down swooped the saber cuttingly. The blade of the sword-cane snapped like a pipe-stem. The vintner flung the broken part at the colonel's head. The latter dodged it and came on, and there was death's intent.

Meantime Carmichael had found a short hop-pole, and with this he took a hand in the contest. The pole was clumsy, but the tough wood was stronger than steel. He hit the saber with good-will. Back came the steel. The colonel did not care whom or what he struck at now. When Carmichael returned the compliment he swung his hop-pole as the old crusaders did their broadswords. And this made short work of the duel. The saber dropped uninjured, but the colonel's arm dangled at his side. He leaned back against the arbor, his teeth set in his lip, for he was in agony. Carmichael flung aside his primitive weapon, his anger abated none.

"You're a fine example of a soldier! Are you mad to attack a man this way? They will break you for this, or my name's not Carmichael. You couldn't leave her in peace, could you? Well, those two kisses will prove expensive."

"I shall kill you for this!"

"Bah! I have fought more times than you have years to your counting," with good Yankee spirit. "But if you think I'll waste my time in fighting a duel with you, you're up the wrong tree."

"Go to the devil!"

"Not just at present; there's too much for me to do. But this is my advice to you: apply for a leave of absence and take the waters of Wiesbaden. They are good for choleric dispositions. Now, I return the compliment: go to the devil yourself, only choose a route that will not cross mine. That's all!"

Gretchen and the vintner had vanished. Carmichael agreed that it was the best thing for them to do. The vintner was no coward, but he was discreet. Somebody might ask questions. So Carmichael returned to the consulate, equally indifferent what the colonel did or where he went. Of the vintner he thought: "The hot-headed young fool, to risk his life like that!" He would see later what he meant in regard to Gretchen. Poor little goose-girl! They would find that there was one man interested enough in her welfare to stand by her. His hands yet stung from the contact of wood against steel, and his hair was damp at the edges. This was a bit of old war-times.

"Are you hurt, Excellency?" asked the clerk solicitously.

"Hurt?"

"Yes. I heard a woman scream and ran to the window. It was a good fight. But that fellow-*ach!* To run away and leave you, an outsider, to fight his battle!"

"He would have been sliced in two if I hadn't come to the front. A hop-pole isn't half bad. I'll bet that lady's man has a bad arm for some time to come. As for the vintner, he had good reasons for taking to his heels."

"Good reasons?" But there was a sly look in the clerk's eyes.

"No questions, if you please. And tell no one, mind, what has taken place."

"Very well, Excellency." And quietly the clerk returned to

his table of figures. But later he intended to write a letter, unsigned, to his serene highness.

Carmichael, scowling, undertook to answer his mail, but not with any remarkable brilliancy or coherency.

And in this condition of mind Grumbach found him; Grumbach, accompanied by the old clock-mender from across the way, and a Gipsy Carmichael had never seen before.

"What's up, Hans?"

"Tell your clerk to leave us," said Grumbach, his face as barren of expression as a rock.

"Something serious, eh?" Carmichael dismissed the clerk, telling him to return after the noon hour. "Now, then," he said, "what is the trouble?"

"I have already spoken to you about it," Grumbach returned. "The matter has gone badly. But I am here to ask a favor, a great favor, one that will need all your diplomacy to gain for me."

"Ah"

"For myself I ask nothing. A horrible blunder has been made. You will go to the grand duke and ask immunity for this Gipsy and this clock-mender, as witnesses to the disclosure which I shall make to his highness. Without this immunity my lips will be sealed for ever. As I said, I ask nothing for myself, nothing. There has been a great blunder and a great wrong, too; but God sent me here to right it. Will you do this?"

"But I must know - ," began Carmichael.

"You will know everything, once you obtain this concession from the duke."

"But why don't you want immunity for yourself?"

"There must be some one for the duke to punish," heroically; "otherwise he will refuse."

"Still, suppose I bargain for you, too?"

"When you tell him my name is Breunner there will be no bargaining."

"What has this clock-mender to do with the case?"

"He is Count von Arnsberg."

"By George! And this Gipsy?"

"The man who bribed me. Arnsberg is an innocent man; but this has to be proved, and you are going to help us prove it."

All this was in English; the Gipsy and the former chancellor understood little or nothing.

"I will do what I can, Hans, and I will let you know the result after dinner to-night."

"That will be enough. But unless he concedes, do not tell him our names. That would be ruin and nothing gained."

"You have me a bit dazed," Carmichael admitted. "I ought to know what this blunder is, to have something to stand on."

Grumbach shook his head. "Later every question will be answered. And remember, at this interview Herbeck must not be present. It will have to be broken to him gently."

"Very well; I promise to see his highness this afternoon."

Grumbach translated the substance of this dialogue to his companions. They approved. The three of them solemnly trooped out, leaving Carmichael bewildered. Alone, his mind searched a thousand channels, but these were blind and led nowhere. Blunder, wrong? What did Grumbach mean by that? What kind of a blunder, and who was innocently wronged? No use! And while he was thus racking his mind he heard steps on the stairs. These steps were hurried. The door above shut noisily.

"By George! I'll attend to that this minute. We'll see what stuff this yellow-haired boy is made of."

He mounted the stairs without sound. He grasped the handle of the door, boldly pushed it open, and entered, closing the door and placing his back against it.

The instant he saw the intruder the vintner snatched a pistol from the drawer in the table and leveled it at Carmichael.

"Surely your majesty will not shoot an old friend?"

CHAPTER XX

THE KING

The vintner slowly lowered the pistol till it touched the table; then he released it.

"That is better, your Majesty."

"Why do you call me that?"

"Certainly I do not utter it as a compliment," retorted Carmichael dryly.

"You speak positively."

"With absolute authority on the subject, sire. Your face was familiar, but I failed at first to place it rightly. It was only after you had duped me into going after the veiled lady that I had any real suspicion. You are Frederick Leopold of Jugendheit."

"I shall not deny it further," proudly. "And take care how you speak to me, since I admit my identity."

"Oho!" Carmichael gave rein to his laughter. "This is Ehrenstein; here I shall talk to you as I please."

Harold MacGrath

The king reddened, and his hand closed again over the pistol.

"I have saved your majesty twice from death. You force me to recall it to your mind."

The king had the grace to lower his eyes.

"The first time was at Bonn. Don't you recollect the day when an American took you out of the Rhine, an American who did not trouble himself to come round and ask for your thanks, who, in truth, did not learn till days after what an important person you were, or were going to be?" There was a bite in every word, for Carmichael felt that he had been ill-treated.

"For that moment, Herr, I thank you."

"And for that in the garden below?"

"For that also. Now, why are you here? You have not come for the purpose of recalling these two disagreeable incidents to my mind."

"No." Carmichael went over to the table, his jaws set and no kindly spirit in his eyes. "No, I have another purpose." He bent over the table, and with his face close to that of the king, "I demand to know what your intentions are toward that friendless goose-girl."

"And what is that to you?" said the king, the smoke of anger in his eyes.

"It is this much: if you have acted toward her otherwise than honorably - Well!"

"Go on; you interest me!"

"Well, I promise to break every bone in your kingly body. In this room it is man to man; I recognize no king, only the physical being."

The king pushed aside the table, furious. No living being had ever spoken to him like that before. He swung the flat of his hand toward Carmichael's face. The latter caught the hand by the wrist and bore down upon it. The king was no weakling. There was a struggle, and Carmichael found himself well occupied for a time. But his age and build were in his favor, and presently he jammed the king to the wall and pinioned his arms.

"There! Will you be patient for a moment?"

"You shall die for this insult!" said the king, as quietly as his hard breathing would allow. He saw flashes of red between his face and the other's.

"I have heard that before. But how?" banteringly.

"I will waive my crown; man to man!"

"Sword-sticks, sabers or hop-poles? Come," savagely, "what do you mean by the goose-girl?"

So intent on the struggle were they that neither heard the door open and close.

"Yes, my dear nephew; what do you mean by Gretchen?"

Carmichael released the king, and with feline quickness stooped and secured the pistol which had fallen to the floor. Not sure of the new arrival's purpose, he backed to the wall. He knew the voice and he recognized its owner.

"Put it in your pocket, Mr. Carmichael. And let us finish this discussion in English, since there are many ears about the place."

"His royal highness?" murmured the king.

"Yes, sire! True to life!"

Carmichael dropped the pistol into a pocket, and the king smoothed down his crumpled sleeves.

"A fine comedy!" cried Herr Ludwig jovially, folding his arms over his deep chest. "A rollicking adventure! Where's the story-book to match it? A kingdom, working in the dark, headless; fine reading for these sneaking journalists! Thunder and blazes!" with an amiability which had behind it a good leaven of despair. "Well, nephew, you have not as yet answered either Mr. Carmichael's question or my own. What do you mean by Gretchen?"

"I love her," nobly. "And well for you, my uncle, that you come as you do. I would have married her! Wrong her? What was a crown to me who, till now, have never worn one save in speech? *You* have been the king."

"Bodies must have heads, kingdoms must have kings. I have tried an experiment, and this is the result. I wanted you to be a man, a human man; I wanted you to grow up unfettered by power; I wanted you to mingle with peoples, here and there, so, when you became their head physician, you could ably minister to their political diseases. And all this fine ambition tumbles down before the wooden shoes of a pretty goose-girl. Nothing makes so good a philosopher as a series of blunders and mistakes. I am beaten; I admit it. I did my best to save you from this tangle; but it was written that you should put your foot in it. But on top of this you have made a greater mistake than you dream of, nephew. The Princess Hildegarde is as fine a woman as ever your Gretchen. Mr. Carmichael will agree to that," maliciously.

Carmichael gave no sign that he understood; but there was no mistaking the prince regent's inference, however. The recipient of this compliment stubbornly refused to give the prince the satisfaction of seeing how neatly the barb had gone home.

"But, Mr. Carmichael, what is *your* interest in Gretchen?"

Carmichael trembled with joy. Here was an opening for a double shot. "My interest in her is better than yours, for I have not asked her to become a king's mistress."

His royal highness bit his lip.

"Uncle!" cried the king, horrified at this revelation.

"Mr. Carmichael evidently has applied his ear to some keyhole."

"No, thank you! The window was open. My clerk heard you plainly."

"Uncle, is this damnable thing true?"

"Yes. What would you? You were determined to make a fool of yourself. But rest easy. She is ignorant where this offer came from, and, moreover, she spurned it, as Mr. Carmichael's clerk will affirm. Oh, Gretchen is a fine little woman, and I would to God she was of your station!" And the mask fell from the regent's face, leaving it bitter and careworn. "Our presence is known in Dreiberg; it has been known for three days at least. And in coming up here I had another errand. Oh, I haven't forgotten it. In the street there are at least ten soldiers under the sub-chief of the police; rather a curious conjunction."

The king turned white. So it had come at last!

Carmichael ran to the rear window. He shrugged. "There's half a dozen in the garden, too."

"Is there any way to the roofs?"

"None that would serve you."

"Mr. Carmichael," said the king, offering his hand, his handsome face kindly and without rancor, "I should be an ungrateful wretch if I did not ask your full pardon. I am indebted to you twice for my life, little as it amounts to. And in my kingdom you will always be welcome. Will you accept my hand, as one man to another?"

"With happiness, your Majesty. And I ask that you pardon my own hasty words."

"Thank you."

"He is only young," sighed Ludwig.

The king emptied the drawer, put the contents in his pack, tied the strings, and put it under his arm.

"What are you going to do?" asked the uncle, vaguely perturbed.

"I am going down to the soldiers. I am no longer a vintner, I am a king!" And he said this in a manner truly royal.

"*Gott!*" burst from the prince regent. "This boy has marrow in his bones, after all!"

"As you will find, dear uncle, the day after the coronation. You will, of course, go down to them with me?"

"As I am your uncle! But the incarceration will not be long," Ludwig grumbled. "There are ten thousand troops on the other side of the passes, and they have been there ever since I learned that you had gone a-wooing."

"Ten thousand? Well, they shall stay there," said the king determinedly. "I shall not begin my reign with war. I am in the wrong; I had no business to be here. Technically I have broken the treaty, though not in spirit."

"What will you do?"

"Tell the duke the truth. He will not dare go far."

"He will be a good politician, too," said Ludwig, with a smile of approval at Carmichael. "No, boy, there will be no war. And yet I was prepared for it; nor was I wrong in doing so. Already, but for Herbeck, there would be plenty of fighting in the passes. *Ach!* Could you but see the princess!"

"I have seen her," replied the king. "Heaven would have been kinder had I seen her months ago."

"Say to his serene highness, then, that you are willing to marry her."

"I'm afraid you do not understand, uncle," the king replied sadly. "I have the supreme happiness to love and to be loved. Of that nothing can rob me. And for some time to come, uncle mine, I shall treasure that happiness."

"And the little Gretchen?"

"Yes, yes! I have been a scoundrel." And the king's eyes grew moist. "You are happy, Mr. Carmichael; you have no crown to weigh against your love."

"Has he not?" mocked Ludwig.

"That, uncle, is neither kind nor gallant."

And from that moment Carmichael's heart warmed toward the young man, whose sorrow was greater than his own. For the king was giving up the woman who loved him, while Carmichael was only giving up the woman he loved, which is a distinction.

"I ask Mr. Carmichael's pardon," said Prince Ludwig frankly. "But my temper has been sadly tried. Will you grant me a favor?"

"If it is in my power," said Carmichael.

"Go at once to our embassy and notify them what has taken place."

"I will do that at once. If only I could find some way for you to escape!"

"There is none," said the king. "Come, uncle; let us see what is going on down-stairs."

Carmichael followed them down.

"There they are, men!" cried the sub-chief. "You are under arrest!"

"I am the king of Jugendheit," calmly announced Frederick Leopold. "Will you subject me to public arrest?"

"And I," said the uncle, "am Ludwig, prince regent. Let us go to prison as quickly as possible, blockheads!"

The sub-chief laughed uproariously, and even the disciplined soldiers smiled. The king of Jugendheit and the prince regent! This was a good joke, indeed!

"Your majesty and your royal highness," said the sub-chief, his eyes twinkling, "will do me, a poor sub-chief of the police, the honor of accompanying me to the Stein-schloss."

"Lead on, lead on!" cried Ludwig. "But wait! I forgot. There can be no harm in asking why we are arrested."

"You are accused of being military spies from Jugendheit. That is sufficient for the present."

"Frederick, they do not believe us. So much the better!" Ludwig pursed his lips into a whistle.

"May I retain this bundle?" inquired the king.

"Yes. I know what is in it. Forward, march!"

The soldiers formed into a square, and in the center the prisoners were placed. Carmichael made as though to protest, but Prince Ludwig signed for him to be silent.

"Remember!" he said.

The king looked in vain for Gretchen. Then he beckoned to Carmichael, and whispered brokenly: "If you see her, do not tell her what has happened. Better to let her think that I have gone. And she will see nothing in the arrest of the king of Jugendheit."

"I promise."

The troop marched along the street, followed by many curious ones, and many heads popped in and out of the gabled windows. Carmichael watched them till they veered round a corner, and then he returned to the consulate. There he left a note for the clerk, telling him that he would not be in the office again that day. Directly after, he hurried off to the Jugendheit embassy.

An hour later Gretchen appeared before Fraeu Bauer. Gretchen had gone home immediately after the termination of the fight in the garden. It had been the will of her lord and master for her to remain at home throughout the day; but this she could not do. She was worried.

"He was not hurt, Fraeu?" she asked timidly.

"Oh, no! The two of them gave themselves up readily. They are snug in the Stein-schloss by this time."

"The Stein-schloss!" Gretchen blanched. "Holy Mother, what has happened?"

"Why, your vintner and Herr Ludwig were arrested an hour ago, accused of being spies from Jugendheit."

"It is a lie!" cried Gretchen hollowly. She groped blindly for the door.

"Where are you going, Gretchen?" Fraeu Bauer inquired anxiously.

"To her highness! She will save him!"

Her highness was dreaming. She had fallen into this habit of late. A flame in the fireplace, a cloud in the sky, a dash of rain on the window, all these drew her fancy. What the heart wishes the mind will dream. Sunshine was without, clear, brilliant; shadow was within, mellow, nebulous. But to-day her dream was short. A maid of honor announced that the young woman Gretchen sought her presence.

"Admit her. She will be a tonic," said Hildegarde.

Gretchen appeared, red-eyed and disheveled. Instantly she flung herself at the feet of the princess.

"Why, Gretchen!"

"They will not let me see him, Highness!" Gretchen choked.

"What has happened, child?"

"They have arrested him as a spy from Jugendheit, and he is innocent. Save him, Highness!"

"How can I save him?"

"He is not a spy."

"That must be proved, Gretchen. I can not go to the Stein-schloss and order them to liberate him." She lifted Gretchen to her feet.

"I have been there, and they will not let me see him. I love him so!"

"I can arrange that for you. I will go with you myself to

the prison."

"Thanks, Highness, thanks!" Gretchen was hysterical.

The Stein-schloss had been the feudal keep; now it served as the city prison. Its grim gray stones were battle-scarred and time-worn; a place of deep dungeons, huge bolts and bars, and narrow slits in the stone for windows. The prison was both civil and military, but was patrolled and sentineled by soldiers. The king and his uncle had been given adjoining cells on the ground floor. These cells were dry, and light entered from the modern windows in the wall of the corridor. The princess and her protegee were admitted without objection. The sergeant in charge of that floor even permitted them to go into the corridor unattended.

Voices.

"Hush!" whispered her highness, pressing Gretchen's arm.

"*Ach!* Wail, dear nephew, beat your hands upon the bars, curse, waste your breath on stone. Did I not warn you against this very thing when you proposed this mad junket? Well, there are two of us. A fine scandal! They will laugh at us for months to come."

"Woe to the duke for this affront!"

Gretchen started to speak, but the princess quickly put her hand over the goose-girl's mouth.

"Ha! So war is gathering in your veins?"

"I will have revenge for this!"

"Good! Bang - bang! Slash and cut! War is a great invention -

on paper. Come, my boy; you were sensible enough when they brought us here. Control yourself. Be a king in all the word implies. For my part, I begin to see."

"And what do you see?"

"I see that the duke knows who we are, even if his police do not. He will keep us here a day or two, and then magnanimously liberate us with profuse apologies. We shall be escorted to the frontier with honors. His highness loves a jest too well to let this chance escape. Besides, I see in the glass the fine Italian hand of Herbeck. I have always heard that he was a great statesman. Swallow your wrath, even if your tongue goes down with it."

"Gretchen, Gretchen!" said the king.

Gretchen could stand it no longer. She wrenched herself free from the grasp of the princess, who, with pitying heart, understood all now. Poor unhappy Gretchen!

"Here I am, Leopold!" the goose-girl cried, pressing her body against the bars and thrusting her hands through them.

"The devil!" murmured the man in the other cell.

"You here, Gretchen?" The king covered her hands with passionate kisses.

"Yes, yes! They have made a dreadful mistake. You are no spy from Jugendheit."

"No, Gretchen," said the voice from the next cell. "He is far worse than that. He is the king, Gretchen, the king."

"Uncle!" in anguish.

"Let us have it over with," replied Prince Ludwig sadly.

"The king?" Gretchen laughed shrilly. "What jest is this, Leopold?"

The king, still holding her hands, looked down.

"Leopold?" plaintively.

Still he did not speak, still he averted his head. But God knew that his heart was on the rack.

The princess, remaining in the background, not daring to interfere, felt the smart of tears in her eyes. Ah, the poor tender little goose-girl! The pity of it! This king was a scoundrel.

"Leo, look at me! You are laughing! Why, did we not work together in the vineyards, and did we not plan for the future? *Ah*, yes! You are a king only to me. I see. But it is a cruel jest, Leopold. Smile at me! Say something!" Gretchen was hanging to the bars now; her body, held in the vise of growing terror, was almost a dead weight.

"Gretchen, forgive me!" despairingly.

"He asks me to forgive him!" dully. "For what?"

"For being a villain! Yes," his voice keen with agony. "I *am* the king of Jugendheit. But am I less a man for that? Ah, God help me, I have a right to love like other men! Do not doubt me, Gretchen; do not think that I played with you. I love you better than my crown, better than my honor!"

"Take care, nephew!" came Prince Ludwig's warning. "Some one else is near."

"I care not! Before all the world I would gladly proclaim it. I love her. I swear that I shall never marry, that my heart is breaking! Gretchen, Gretchen! My God, she is falling! Help her!" wildly; and he shook the bars with supernatural strength till his hands were bleeding.

But Gretchen did not answer.

CHAPTER XXI

TWIN LOCKETS

Carmichael tramped about his room, restless, uneasy, starting at sounds. Half a dozen times his cigar had gone out, and burned matches lay scattered on the floor. He was waiting for Grumbach and his confreres. Now he looked out of a window, now he spun the leaves of a book, now he sat down, got up, and tramped again. Anything but this suspense. A full day! The duel in the *Biergarten*; the king of Jugendheit and the prince regent in the Stein-schloss; the flight of the ambassador to the palace, more like a madman than one noted for his calm and circumspection; Gretchen carried into the palace in a dead faint, and her highness weeping; the duke in a rage and brought over only after the hardest struggle Carmichael had ever experienced. And deeper, firmer, became his belief and conviction that Grumbach's affair vitally concerned her highness. What blunder had been made? He would soon know. He welcomed the knock on his door. Grumbach came in, carrying under his arm a small bundle. He was pale but serene, like a man who had put his worldly affairs in order.

"Well, Captain, what did his Highness say?"

"Where are your companions?"

"They are waiting outside."

"The duke agrees. He will give us an audience at eight-thirty. I had a time of it!"

"Did you mention my name

"No. I went roundabout. I also obtained his promise to say nothing to Herbeck till the interview was over. Again he demurred, but his curiosity saved the day. Now, Hans, the full story."

Grumbach spread out on the bed the contents of the bundle.

"Look at these and tell me what you see, Captain."

Carmichael inspected the little yellow shoes. He turned them over and over in his hand. He shook out the folds of the little cloak, and the locket fell on the bed.

"When did you get this?" he cried excitedly. "It is her highness'!"

"So it is, Captain; but I have carried it about me all these years."

"What?"

"Yes, Captain. Count von Herbeck is a great statesman, but he made a terrible mistake this time. Listen. As sure as we are in this room together, I believe that she whom we call the princess is not the daughter of the grand duke."

Carmichael sat down on the edge of the bed, numb and without any clear idea where he was. From the stony look on his face, Grumbach might have carried the head of Medusa in his hand. The blood beat into his head with many strange noises. But by and by the world became clearer and brighter till all things took on the rosal tint of dawn. Free! If she was not a princess, she was free, free!

The duke allowed the quartet to remain standing for some time. He strode up and down before them, his eyes straining at the floor, his hands behind his back. He was in fatigue-dress, and only the star of Ehrenstein glittered on his breast. He was never without this order. All at once he whirled round, and as a sailor plunges the lead into the sea, so he plumbed the very deeps of their eyes as if he would see beforehand what strange things were at work in their souls. "I do not recognize any of these persons," he said to Carmichael.

"Your highness does not recognize me, then?" asked the clock-mender.

"Come closer," commanded the duke. The clock-mender obeyed. "Take off those spectacles." The duke scanned the features, and over his own came the dawn of recollection. "Your eyes, your nose - Arnsberg, here and alive? Oh, this is too good to be true!" The duke reached out toward the bell, but Carmichael interposed.

"Your highness will remember," he warned.

"Ha! So you have trapped me blindly? I begin to understand. Who is this fellow Grumbach? Did I offer immunity to him?"

"I am Hans Breunner, Highness, and I ask for nothing."

"Breunner? Breunner? Hans Breunner, brother of Hermann, and you put yourself into my hands?" The tone developed into a suppressed roar. The duke took hold of Hans by the shoulders and drew him close. "You dog! So you ask for nothing? It shall be given to you. To-morrow morning I shall have you shot! Hans Breunner! God is good to me this night! Thanks, Herr Carmichael, a thousand thanks! And I need not ask who that damnable scoundrel is who has the black face and heart of a Gipsy. When I recollect what I have suffered at your hands! If only the late king were here, my joy would be complete!"

"Your Highness," said Von Arnsberg quietly, "all I have left in the world are these two withered hands, and may God cut them off if they ever wronged you in any act. I am innocent. Those letters purported to have been written by me were forgeries. I could not prove this, so I have been outlawed, with the sentence of death over my head. But to-night I shall leave this palace a free man, and you shall ask pardon for the wrong you have done me."

There was no fear in the voice; there was nothing but confidence. The duke glared at the speaker somberly, recalling what Herbeck had often said.

"What you say still remains to be proved. Now, what is at the bottom of all this?" was the demand. "You men have not obtained this interview for the sake of affirming your innocence. Herr Carmichael, here, declared to me on honor that you were in possession of a great secret. Out with it, without any more useless recrimination."

Hans replied not in words but in actions. He crossed the room to the duke's desk and spread out his treasures under the flickering candlelight. The duke, with a cry of terror, sprang toward the secret drawer. His first thought was that the shoes and cloak, upon which only his eyes ever rested now, had been stolen. He straightened. Nothing was missing.

He glanced from face to face, from the articles on the desk to those in the drawer. He was overwhelmed. But he steadied himself; it was no moment for physical weakness. Slowly, ignoring every one, he came back to the desk and fingered the locket. Just then it was exceedingly quiet in the room, save that each man heard the quick breathing of his neighbor. The duke opened the locket, looked long and steadfastly at the portrait, and shut it. Then he went to the drawer again and returned with the counterparts. He laid them side by side. The likeness was perfect in all details.

"Carmichael," he said, "will you please help me? My eyes are growing old. Do I see these things, or do I not? And if I do, which is mine, and what does this signify?" The tremor in his voice was audible.

Grumbach answered. "This, Highness. I took these from the little princess with my own hands. They have never been out of my keeping. Those you have I know nothing about."

The duke rubbed his eyes. "My daughter?"

"The Princess Hildegarde is not your daughter, Highness," said Hans solemnly.

"*Gott*!" The duke smote the desk in despair, a despair which wrung the hearts of those who witnessed it. "Herbeck! I must send for Herbeck!"

"Not yet, Highness; later," Grumbach said.

"But if not Hildegarde - I believe I must be growing mad!"

"Patience, your Highness!" said Carmichael.

"Patience!" wearily. "You say patience when my heart is

dying inside my breast? Patience? Who, then, is this woman I have called my child?"

"God knows, Highness!" Hans stood bowed before this parental agony.

"But what proof have you that she is not? What proof, I say?"

"Would there be two lockets, Highness?"

"More proof than this will be needed. Produce it. Prolong this agony of doubt not another instant."

"Speak," said Hans to the Gipsy, who was viewing the drama with the nonchalance of a spectator rather than a participant.

"Highness," said the Gipsy, bowing, "he speaks truly. He came with us. For fear that the little highness might be recognized as we traveled, we changed her clothes. He took them, together with the locket. One day the soldiers appeared in the distance. We all fled. We lost the little highness, and none of us ever knew what became of her. She wore the costume of my own children."

"We shall produce that in time," said Von Arnsberg.

"Damnable wretch!" said the duke, addressing the Gipsy.

The other shrugged. He had been promised immunity; that was all he cared about, unless it was the bag of silver and gold this old clock-mender had given him a few hours gone.

"I am summoning her highness," said the duke, as he struck the bell.

"And, Highness," added Grumbach, "despatch some one for Gretchen, who lives at number forty the Krumerweg."

"The goose-girl? What does *she* know? Ah, I remember. She is even now with her highness. I shall send for them both."

Gretchen? Carmichael's bewilderment increased. What place had the goose-girl in this tragedy?

"Now, while we are waiting," resumed the duke, his agitation somewhat under control, "the proof, the definite proof!"

"Her highness stumbled one night," said Hans, "and fell upon the fire. I snatched her back, but not before her left arm was badly burned."

The Gipsy nodded. "I saw it, Highness."

And that was why Grumbach went to the military ball with opera-glasses! Carmichael was round-eyed. But Gretchen?

"The Princess Hildegarde has no scar upon either arm," continued Grumbach. "I have seen them. They are without a single flaw."

"More than that," reiterated the duke. "That is not enough."

They became silent. Now and then one or the other stirred. The duke never took his eyes off the door through which her highness would enter.

She came in presently, tender with mercy, an arm supporting Gretchen, who was red-eyed and white.

"You sent for us, father?"

How the word pierced the duke's heart! "Yes, my child," he answered; for it mattered not who she was or whither she had come, he had grown to love her.

"I am sorry you sent for Gretchen," said Hildegarde. "She is ill."

Gretchen sighed. To her the faces of the men were indistinct. And, besides, she was without interest, listless, drooped.

"My child, will you roll up your left sleeve?" said the duke.

"My sleeve?" Hildegarde thoughtfully looked round. Roll up her sleeve? What possessed her father?

"Do so at once."

"I can not roll up this sleeve, father," blushing and a trifle angry at so strange a request.

Hans opened his knife and laid bare her left arm. She uttered a little angry cry. "How dare you?" She tried to cover the arm.

"Let me look at it, Hildegarde," requested the duke.

To him she presented her arm, for she now understood that a serious affair was in progress. But there was neither mole nor scar upon the round and lovely arm.

"Why do you do this, father? What is the meaning?"

No one answered; no one had the heart to answer. Without waiting for the duke to bid him continue, Hans unceremoniously ripped open Gretchen's left sleeve. The ragged scar was visible to them all. And while they grouped round the astonished goose-girl they heard her highness cry out with surprise.

"What is this?" she said, pointing to the two pairs of shoes and the two cloaks. She held up the locket, the twin of which hung round her neck. "Where did these come from?"

"My child," the duke answered, unashamed of his tears, "only God knows as yet what it means; but the outward sign testifies to a strange and horrible blunder. The locket you hold in your hand was taken from you when you were an infant. The one you wear round your neck is, according to the statement of one of these men, not genuine."

"And the significance?" She grew tall, and the torn sleeve fell away from her arm.

"That what is done must be all undone. I know you to be brave. Strengthen your heart, then. I stand before you the most wretched man in all this duchy. These men affirm that I am not your father. They say that you are not my daughter."

"And that Gretchen is!" spoke Hans. His conscience was costing every one something dear.

"I?" Gretchen drew closer to Hildegarde.

The duke studied the portrait of the mother and then the faces of these two girls. Both possessed a resemblance, only it seemed now that Gretchen was nearest to the portrait and Hildegarde nearest to the doubt.

"You say she wore the costume of a Gipsy child when you lost her?" said the duke.

"Yes." Von Arnsberg took from under his coat a small

bundle which he opened with shaking fingers. He had been in the Krumerweg that afternoon.

"Why, those are mine!" exclaimed Gretchen excitedly.

"You see?" said Von Arnsberg. "Would you not like to be a princess, Gretchen?"

A princess? Gretchen's heart fluttered. A princess? She saw the king shaking the bars of his cell; she heard his voice calling out his love for her. A princess? She laid her head on Hildegarde's shoulder. She was weak, and this was some dream.

"But who, then, am I?" asked Hildegarde. There was no sign of weakness here.

Again there was no answer.

"Tell what you know," said Hans to the Gipsy. "Highness, he alone knows the man who brought about all this."

"The archplotter of this damnable conspiracy?" The duke's eyes became alive, his face, his whole body. Every beat of his heart cried out for vengeance. "Who is he? Tell me! Give him to me, man, and all of you shall go free. Give him into these hands. His name!" The duke's hands worked convulsively as if they were already round the throat of this unseen, implacable enemy. He was terrible in this moment.

The Gipsy produced a letter. It had to be held carefully, as it was old and tattered. The duke read it. Beyond that it made the original offer it was worthless. The handwriting was palpably disguised. The duke flung the missive to the floor.

"Fool! Is that all you have? Tell me what you know, man, or

Harold MacGrath

I shall have you shot in the morning, immunity or no immunity! Quick!"

"Highness," said the Gipsy, thoroughly alarmed, "this is how it happened. My band was staying at the time in Dreiberg. We told fortunes and exhibited an Italian puppet-show. The letter came first. I was poor and sometimes desperate. I was to take her away and leave her with strange people."

"Ah!" interrupted the duke, with despairing gesture toward Grumbach, "why did you not leave us all in peace?"

"Highness, a great wrong has been done, and God brought me here to right it."

"You are a brave man," darkly.

"I am in your hands, Highness," sturdily. "In a mad moment I committed a crime. I shall abide by whatever punishment you may inflict."

"Continue," said the duke to the Gipsy.

"Well, Highness, I would not accept till I had talked personally with him. He came at last. His face was hidden and his voice muffled. But this I saw; when he gave me the first half of the money I was certain I should know him again."

"How?"

"By his little finger, Highness."

"His little finger?" Von Arnsberg repeated. The two women, large-eyed and bewildered, clung to each other's hand tensely. These were heart-breaking times. Gretchen's mind, however, absorbed nothing, neither the words nor the picture. Her thoughts revolved round one thing; if she were a princess she could be happy. But the other, from under whose feet all tangible substances seemed to be giving way, she was possessed by two thoughts which surged in her brain like combatants. If not a princess, what was she? If not a princess, she was free. She stole a swift glance at Carmichael, who seemed far removed from the heart of this black business; and had he been looking at her he would have seen the gates opening into Eden.

"What was this little finger like?" asked the duke, shuddering.

"One time it had been cut or mangled."

"The man was tall?"

"Yes, Highness."

The duke silently toyed with the little yellow shoes. Suddenly he laughed; but it was the terrible laughter of a madman. There were death and desolation in it.

"Come, all of you; you, Gretchen, and you, Hildegarde; come, Carmichael, and you, Arnsberg; all of you! Let us go and pay a visit to our good friend, Herbeck!"

CHAPTER XXII

A LITTLE FINGER

The king of Jugendheit, Prince Ludwig, and the chancellor sat in the form of a triangle. Herbeck was making a pyramid of his finger-tips, sometimes touching his chin with his thumbs. His face was cheerful. His royal highness, still in the guise of a mountaineer, sat stiffly in his chair, the expression on his face hardly translatable; that on the king's not at all. He was dressed in the brilliant uniform of a colonel in the Prussian Uhlans, an honor conferred upon him recently by King William. Prior to his advent into the Grand Duchy of Ehrenstein he had been to Berlin. A whim, for which he was now grateful, had cozened him into carrying this uniform along with him on his adventures. It was only after he met Gretchen that there came moments when he forgot he was a king. He was pale. From hour to hour his heart seemed to grow colder and smaller and harder, till it now rested in his breast with the heaviness of a stone, out of which life and the care of living had been squeezed. He rarely spoke, leaving the burden of the conversation to rest upon his uncle's tongue.

"So your royal highness will understand," said Herbeck, "that it was the simplest move I could make, and the safest. Were it known, or had it been known this morning, that the king of Jugendheit and the prince regent had entered Dreiberg in disguise and had been lodged in the Stein-schloss, there would have been a serious riot in the city. So I had you arrested as spies. Presently a closed carriage will convey you to the frontier, and the unfortunate incident will be ended."

"Thanks!" said Prince Ludwig.

"And when you cross the frontier, it would be wise to disperse the troops waiting there for you."

Prince Ludwig smiled. "It was only an army of defense. The duke had nearly twenty thousand men at the maneuvers. I have no desire for war; but, on the other hand, I am always ready for it."

"There will never be any war between us," prophetically. "The duke grows impatient at times, but I can always rouse his sense of justice. You will, of course, pardon the move I made. There will be no publicity. There will be no newspaper notoriety, for the journalists will know nothing of what has really happened."

"For that consideration your excellency has my deepest thanks," replied Prince Ludwig.

"I thought it best to let you go without seeing the duke. The meeting between you two might be painful."

"That also is thoughtful of your excellency," said the king. "I have no desire to see or speak to his highness."

"There is, however, one favor I should like to ask," said the prince.

"Can I grant it?"

"Easily. I wish to leave a sum of money in trust, to be paid to one Gretchen Schwarz, who lives in the Krumerweg. She is ambitious to become a singer. Let nothing stand between her and her desires."

"Granted."

The heart of the king, at the sound of that dear name, suddenly expanded and stifled him. The stiffness went out of his shoulders.

"Ah, this little world of ours, the mistakes and futile schemes we make upon it!" The chancellor dallied with his quill pen. "It was a cynical move of fate that your majesty should see the goose-girl first."

"Enough!" cried the king vehemently. "Let us have no more retrospection, if you please. Moreover, I shall be obliged to you if you will summon at once the carriage which is to take us to the frontier. The situation has been amicably and satisfactorily explained. I see no reason why we should be detained any longer."

"Nor I," added Prince Ludwig. "I am rather weary of these tatters. I should even like a bath."

The three of them were immediately attracted by a singular noise outside in the corridor. The door swung in violently, crashing against the wall and shivering into atoms the Venetian mirror. The king, the prince, and the chancellor were instantly upon their feet. The king clutched the back of his chair with a grip of iron: Gretchen? Her highness? What was Gretchen doing here? Ah, could he have flown! He muttered a curse at the chancellor for the delay. But happily

Gretchen did not see him.

The duke came in first, and he waited till the others were inside; then he shut the door with lesser violence and rushed over to the chancellor.

"Herbeck, you villain!"

The chancellor stared at the Gipsy, at Von Arnsberg, at Grumbach.

"Herbeck, you black scoundrel!" cried the duke. "Can you realize how difficult it is not to take you by the throat and strangle you here and now?"

"He is mad!" said Herbeck, bracing himself against the desk.

"Yes. I *am* mad, but it is the sane madness of a terribly wronged man. Come here, you Gipsy!" The duke seized Herbeck's hand and pressed it down fiercely on the desk. "Look at that and tell me if it is not the hand of a Judas!"

"That is the hand, Highness," said the Gipsy, without hesitation.

The duke flung the hand aside. As he did so something snapped in Herbeck's brain, though at that instant he was not conscious of it.

"It was you, you! It was your hand that wrecked my life, yours! Ah, is there such villainy? Are such men born and do they live? My wife dead, my own heart broken, Arnsberg ruined and disgraced! And these two children: which is mine?"

To the king of Jugendheit the ceiling reeled and the floor

Harold MacGrath

revolved under his feet.

"Villain, what have you to say? What was your purpose?"

How many years, thought Herbeck, had he been preparing for this moment? How long had he been steeling his heart against this very scene? Futile dream! He drew himself together with a supreme effort. He would face this hour as he had always planned to face it. Found out! He looked at his finger, touched it with an impersonal curiosity. He had forgotten all about such a possibility. Where had he read that there is no crime but leaves some evidence, infinitesimally small though it be, which shall lead to the truth? After all, he was glad. The strain, borne so long, was gradually killing him. A little finger, to have stopped the wheel of so great a scheme! Irony!

"Your Highness," he said, his voice soft and strangely clear, "I have been waiting for this hour. So I am found out! How little we know what God intends!"

"You speak of God? You blaspheme!"

"Bear with me for a space. I shall not hold you long."

"But why? What have I done to you that you should wreck all I hold dear?"

"For you I have always had a strong affection, strange as it may sound." Herbeck fumbled with his collar, which was tightening round his throat like a band of hot iron. "I have practically governed this country for sixteen years. In that time I have made it prosperous and happy; I have given you a substantial treasury; I have made you an army; I have brought peace where you would have brought war. To my people God will witness that I have done my duty as I saw it.

One day I fell the victim of a mad dream. And to think that I almost won!"

"And I?" said Hildegarde, her hands clenched and pressed against her bosom. "What have you done to me, who am innocent of any wrong? What have you done to me?"

"You, my child? I have wronged you greatest of all. The wrong I have done to you is irreparable. Ah, have not my arms hungered for the touch of you, my heart ached for the longing of you? To see you day after day, always humble before you, always glad to kiss the back of your hand! Have I not lived in hell, your Highness?" turning to the duke.

"What am I, and who am I?" whispered Hildegarde, her heart almost ceasing to beat.

"I am your father!" simply.

CHAPTER XXIII

HAPPINESS

The grand duke of Ehrenstein beheld the chancellor with that phase of astonishment which leaves the mind unclouded. The violent storm in his heart gave way to a calm, not at all menacing, but tinctured with a profound pity. What a project! What a mind to conceive it, to perfect it down to so small a detail as a jeweler's mark in the gold of the locket! And a little finger to betray it! In a flash he saw vividly all this man had undergone, day by day, unfaltering, unhesitant, forgetting nothing, remembering everything but the one insignificant item which was to overthrow him. He felt that he was confronted with a great problem; what to do with the man?

Prince Ludwig took off his hat. "Herbeck, you are a great politician."

"No, prince," replied Herbeck, with ineffable sadness. "Had I been a great politician I should have succeeded. Ah, give this to my merit; self never entered into this dream. For you, my child, only for you. And so great was this dream that I almost made you a queen! You are my flesh and blood, the child of my wife, whom I loved. She was only a singer in the opera, at Dresden, but her soul was great, like yours. It is a simple story."

Hildegarde did not move, nor had she moved since the revelation. Carmichael, a secret joy in his heart, watched the girl for the slightest swaying, that inevitable prelude to fainting. But Hildegarde was not the kind of woman who faints in the face of a catastrophe, however great it might be. The only sign of life lay in her beautiful eyes, the gaze of which remained unswervingly fixed upon the chancellor's ashen countenance.

"Hildegarde," said the duke, "you shall become my daughter, and you shall dwell here till the end of your days. I will try to right the wrong that has been done to you."

"No, your Highness," she replied. "There is but one place for me, and that is at my father's side." And resolutely she walked to the chancellor's left and her hand stole down and met his firmly. "My father, I forgive you," she said, with quiet dignity.

"They are all wrong, Frederick," whispered Prince Ludwig. "She is as much a princess as the other."

"You forgive me?" The chancellor could not believe his ears.

"Yes, father."

Then, recalling all the child-hunger in his arms and heart, he swept her to his breast convulsively; and the unloosed tears dropped upon her bright head.

"And who am I?" said Gretchen.

"Breunner, you say this little goose-girl is my daughter?"

"I solemnly swear it, Highness. Look into her face again carefully."

Harold MacGrath

The duke did so, a hand on either cheek. He scrutinized every contour, the color of the eyes, the low, broad brow, the curve of the chin. Out of the past he conjured up the mother's face. Yes, beyond any doubt, there was a haunting likeness, and he had never noted it before.

"But who will prove it to the world?" he cried hopelessly, still holding Gretchen's wondering face between his hands.

"I shall prove it," said the king.

"You? And how?"

"I shall marry Gretchen; I shall make her a queen. That will be proof enough."

"A fine stroke, nephew; a bold stroke!" Prince Ludwig laid his hand upon the king's shoulder with rare affection.

"If you accept her without further proof, I, her father, can do no less." And the duke kissed Gretchen on the forehead and led her over to the king, gravely joining their hands.

"Gretchen!" murmured the king.

"I do not know how to act like a princess."

"I shall teach you."

Gretchen laid her head on his breast. She was very tired and much bewildered.

The duke paced the length of the cabinet several times. No one interrupted his meditation.

Back and forth, one hand hanging to the opposite shoulder, the other folding over his chin. Then he paused with abruptness.

"Your Majesty, I regret that your father is not alive to accept my apologies for so baselessly misjudging him. Arnsberg, nothing that I can do will restore these wasted years. But I offer you the portfolio."

"I am only a broken man, your Highness; too old."

"It is my will."

Arnsberg bent his head in submission.

"As for you," said the duke to the Gipsy, "go, and if you ever step this side the frontier again you will be shot out of hand." He stopped again in front of Grumbach. "I promised to have you shot in the morning. That promise holds. But a train leaves for Paris a little after midnight. My advice is for you not to miss it."

"And my father, your Highness?" said Hildegarde bravely.

"Herbeck, your estates are confiscated, your name is struck from the civic and military lists. Have you any ready funds?"

"A little, your Highness."

"Enough to take you for ever out of this part of the world?"

"Yes, your Highness."

"You do not ask to be forgiven, and I like that. I have judges in Dreiberg. I could have you tried and condemned for high treason, shot or imprisoned for life. But to-night I shall not use this prerogative. You have, perhaps, three hours to get your things in order. To-morrow you will be judged and condemned. But you, Hildegarde - "

"No, your Highness; we shall both take the train for Paris. Gretchen, you will be happy."

Gretchen ran and flung herself into Hildegarde's arms; and the two of them wept. Hildegarde pushed Gretchen away gently.

"Come, father, we have so little time."

And this was the sum of the duke's revenge.

* * * * *

It never took Carmichael long to make up his mind definitely. He found his old friend the cabman in the Platz, and they drove like mad to the consulate. An hour here sufficed to close his diplomatic career and seal it hermetically. The clerk, however, would go on like Tennyson's brook, for ever and for ever. Next he went to the residence of his banker in the Koenig Strasse and got together all his available funds. Eleven o'clock found him in his rooms at the Grand Hotel, feverishly packing his trunk and bag. Paris! He would go, also, even if they passed on to the remote ends of the world.

The train stood waiting in the gloomy Bahnhof. The guards patrolled the platform. Presently three men came out of the station door. Two were officers; the third, Colonel von Wallenstein, was in civilian dress. He was sullen and depressed.

Said one of the officers: "And it is the express command of General Ducwitz that you will return here under the pain of death. Is that explicit?"

"It is." The colonel got into his compartment and slammed the door viciously.

In the next compartment sat Grumbach. He was smoking his faithful pipe. He was, withal, content. This was far more satisfactory than standing up before the firing-line. And, besides, he had made history in Ehrenstein that night; they would not forget the name of Breunner right away. To America, with a clean slate and a reposeful conscience; it was more than he had any reasonable right to expect. Tekla! He laughed sardonically. She was no doubt sound asleep by this time, and the end of the chapter would never be written for her. What fools these young men a-courting were! War and famine and pestilence; did these not always follow at the heels of women?

As the station-master's bell rang, the door opened and a man jumped in. He tossed his bag into the corner and plumped down in the seat.

"Captain?"

"You, Hans?"

"Yes. Where are you going?"

"I am weary of Dreiberg, so I am taking a little vacation."

"For how long?" suspiciously.

"Oh, for ever so long!" evasively. And Carmichael lifted his feet to the opposite seat and prepared to go to sleep.

Hans said nothing more. He was full of wisdom. He had an idea. The fleeing chancellor and his daughter were on the train, and he was certain that his friend Carmichael knew it.

The lights of the city presently vanished, and the long journey began, through the great clefts in the mountains, over gorges, across rivers, along wide valleys, and into the mountains again; a journey of nearly seventy hours. At each stop Carmichael got out, and every time he returned Hans could read disappointment on his face. Still he said nothing. He was an admirable comrade.

By the aid of certain small briberies on the train and in Paris Carmichael gathered, bit by bit, that the destination of the woman he loved was America. But never once did he set eyes upon her till she and her father mounted the gang-plank to the vessel which was to carry them across the wide Atlantic. The change in Herbeck was pitiable. His face had aged twenty years in these sixty odd hours. His clothes, the same he had worn that ever-memorable night, hung loosely about his gaunt frame, and there was a vacancy in his eyes which was eloquent of mental collapse. The girl quietly and tenderly guided him to the deck and thence to his stateroom. Carmichael abided his time.

A French newspaper contained a full account of Herbeck's *coup* and his subsequent flight. It also recounted the excitement of the following day, the appearance of Gretchen on the steps of the palace, and the great shouting of the people as they acclaimed her the queen of Jugendheit.

The second day out Carmichael's first opportunity came. He discovered Herbeck and his daughter leaning against the rail. He watched them uneasily, wondering how he might approach without startling her. At last he keyed up his courage.

"Good morning, your Highness," he stammered, and inwardly cursed his stupidity.

At the sound of his voice she turned, and there was no mistaking the gladness in her eyes.

"Mr. Carmichael?"

"Yes. I was surprised to learn that you were taking the same boat as myself."

How clumsy he was! she thought. For she had known his every move since the train drew out of Dreiberg.

"Father, here is our friend, Herr Carmichael."

"Carmichael?" said Herbeck slowly.. "Ah, yes. Good morning."

And Carmichael instantly comprehended that his name recalled nothing to the other man's remembrance.

"You are returning to America?" she asked.

"For good, perhaps. To tell the truth, I ran away, deserted my post, though technically I have already resigned. But America has been calling me for some days. You have never been to sea before?"

"No; it is all marvelous and strange to me."

"Let us walk, my child," said Herbeck.

"You will excuse me, Mr. Carmichael?" she said. Never more the rides in the fair mornings. Never more the beautiful gardens, the music, the galloping of soldiers who drew their sabers whenever they passed her. Never more any of these things.

Harold MacGrath

"Can I be of any assistance?" he said, in an undertone.

"No," sadly.

The days, more or less monotonous, went past. Sometimes he saw her alone on deck, but only for a little while. Her father was slowly improving, but with this improvement came the natural desire for seclusion; so he came on deck only at night.

The night on which the vessel bore into the moist, warm air of the Gulf Stream was full of moonshine, of smooth, phosphorescent billows. Herbeck had gone below. The girl leaned over the rail, alone and lonely. And Carmichael, seeing her, could no longer still the desire in his heart. He came up to her.

"See!" she exclaimed, pointing to the little eddies of foam speeding along the hull. "Do you know what they remind me of? Mermaids' fingers, grasping and clutching at the boat as if to drag it down below."

How beautiful she was with the frost of moonlight on her hair!

"You must not talk like that," he admonished.

"I am very unhappy."

"And when you say that you make me so, too."

"Why?" She had spoken the word at last.

"Do you remember the night you dropped your fan?" leaning so closely toward her that his arm pressed against hers.

"I remember."

"You put that word then. In honor I dared not answer. You were a princess! I was only a soldier of fortune. But now that you are in trouble, now that you have need of me, I may answer. I may tell you now why, why I have thrown ambition and future to the winds, why I am here at your side to-night. Need I tell you? Do you not know, and have you not known? Am I cruel to speak of love in the moment of your great affliction? Well, I must be cruel. I love you! Faithfully and loyally, now and hereafter, through this sad day into happier ones. I ask nothing for this love I offer; I ask only that I may use it in your service, in good times or bad."

"Ask what you will," she whispered. "I am happy now!"

Harold MacGrath

ABOUT THE AUTHOR

Harold MacGrath (September 4, 1871 - October 30, 1932) was a bestselling American novelist, short story writer, and screenwriter.

Also known occasionally as Harold McGrath, he was born in Syracuse, New York. As a young man, he worked as a reporter and columnist on the Syracuse Herald newspaper until the late 1890s when he published his first novel, a romance titled "Arms and the Woman." According to the New York Times, his next book, "The Puppet Crown," was the No.7 bestselling book in the United States for all of 1901. From that point on, MacGrath never looked back, writing novels for the mass market about love, adventure, mystery, spies, and the like at an average rate of more than one a year. He would have three more of his books that were among the top ten bestselling books of the year. At the same time, he penned a number of short stories for major American magazines such as The Saturday Evening Post, Ladies Home Journal, and Red Book magazine. Several of MacGrath's novels were serialized in these magazines and contributing to them was something he would continue to do until his death in 1932.

Choose from Thousands of 1stWorldLibrary Classics By

A. M. Barnard
Ada Leverson
Adolphus William Ward
Aesop
Agatha Christie
Alexander Aaronsohn
Alexander Kielland
Alexandre Dumas
Alfred Gatty
Alfred Ollivant
Alice Duer Miller
Alice Turner Curtis
Alice Dunbar
Allen Chapman
Alleyne Ireland
Ambrose Bierce
Amelia E. Barr
Amory H. Bradford
Andrew Lang
Andrew McFarland Davis
Andy Adams
Angela Brazil
Anna Alice Chapin
Anna Sewell
Annie Besant
Annie Hamilton Donnell
Annie Payson Call
Annie Roe Carr
Annonaymous
Anton Chekhov
Archibald Lee Fletcher
Arnold Bennett
Arthur C. Benson
Arthur Conan Doyle
Arthur M. Winfield
Arthur Ransome
Arthur Schnitzler
Arthur Train
Atticus
B.H. Baden-Powell
B. M. Bower
B. C. Chatterjee
Baroness Emmuska Orczy
Baroness Orczy
Basil King
Bayard Taylor
Ben Macomber
Bertha Muzzy Bower
Bjornstjerne Bjornson

Booth Tarkington
Boyd Cable
Bram Stoker
C. Collodi
C. E. Orr
C. M. Ingleby
Carolyn Wells
Catherine Parr Traill
Charles A. Eastman
Charles Amory Beach
Charles Dickens
Charles Dudley Warner
Charles Farrar Browne
Charles Ives
Charles Kingsley
Charles Klein
Charles Hanson Towne
Charles Lathrop Pack
Charles Romyn Dake
Charles Whibley
Charles Willing Beale
Charlotte M. Braeme
Charlotte M. Yonge
Charlotte Perkins Stetson
Clair W. Hayes
Clarence Day Jr.
Clarence E. Mulford
Clemence Housman
Confucius
Coningsby Dawson
Cornelis DeWitt Wilcox
Cyril Burleigh
D. H. Lawrence
Daniel Defoe
David Garnett
Dinah Craik
Don Carlos Janes
Donald Keyhoe
Dorothy Kilner
Dougan Clark
Douglas Fairbanks
E. Nesbit
E. P. Roe
E. Phillips Oppenheim
E. S. Brooks
Earl Barnes
Edgar Rice Burroughs
Edith Van Dyne
Edith Wharton

Edward Everett Hale
Edward J. O'Biren
Edward S. Ellis
Edwin L. Arnold
Eleanor Atkins
Eleanor Hallowell Abbott
Eliot Gregory
Elizabeth Gaskell
Elizabeth McCracken
Elizabeth Von Arnim
Ellem Key
Emerson Hough
Emilie F. Carlen
Emily Bronte
Emily Dickinson
Enid Bagnold
Enilor Macartney Lane
Erasmus W. Jones
Ernie Howard Pie
Ethel May Dell
Ethel Turner
Ethel Watts Mumford
Eugene Sue
Eugenie Foa
Eugene Wood
Eustace Hale Ball
Evelyn Everett-green
Everard Cotes
F. H. Cheley
F. J. Cross
F. Marion Crawford
Fannie E. Newberry
Federick Austin Ogg
Ferdinand Ossendowski
Fergus Hume
Florence A. Kilpatrick
Fremont B. Deering
Francis Bacon
Francis Darwin
Frances Hodgson Burnett
Frances Parkinson Keyes
Frank Gee Patchin
Frank Harris
Frank Jewett Mather
Frank L. Packard
Frank V. Webster
Frederic Stewart Isham
Frederick Trevor Hill
Frederick Winslow Taylor

Friedrich Kerst
Friedrich Nietzsche
Fyodor Dostoyevsky
G.A. Henty
G.K. Chesterton
Gabrielle E. Jackson
Garrett P. Serviss
Gaston Leroux
George A. Warren
George Ade
Geroge Bernard Shaw
George Cary Eggleston
George Durston
George Ebers
George Eliot
George Gissing
George MacDonald
George Meredith
George Orwell
George Sylvester Viereck
George Tucker
George W. Cable
George Wharton James
Gertrude Atherton
Gordon Casserly
Grace E. King
Grace Gallatin
Grace Greenwood
Grant Allen
Guillermo A. Sherwell
Gulielma Zollinger
Gustav Flaubert
H. A. Cody
H. B. Irving
H.C. Bailey
H. G. Wells
H. H. Munro
H. Irving Hancock
H. R. Naylor
H. Rider Haggard
H. W. C. Davis
Haldeman Julius
Hall Caine
Hamilton Wright Mabie
Hans Christian Andersen
Harold Avery
Harold McGrath
Harriet Beecher Stowe
Harry Castlemon
Harry Coghill
Harry Houidini

Hayden Carruth
Helent Hunt Jackson
Helen Nicolay
Hendrik Conscience
Hendy David Thoreau
Henri Barbusse
Henrik Ibsen
Henry Adams
Henry Ford
Henry Frost
Henry James
Henry Jones Ford
Henry Seton Merriman
Henry W Longfellow
Herbert A. Giles
Herbert Carter
Herbert N. Casson
Herman Hesse
Hildegard G. Frey
Homer
Honore De Balzac
Horace B. Day
Horace Walpole
Horatio Alger Jr.
Howard Pyle
Howard R. Garis
Hugh Lofting
Hugh Walpole
Humphry Ward
Ian Maclaren
Inez Haynes Gillmore
Irving Bacheller
Isabel Cecilia Williams
Isabel Hornibrook
Israel Abrahams
Ivan Turgenev
J.G.Austin
J. Henri Fabre
J. M. Barrie
J. M. Walsh
J. Macdonald Oxley
J. R. Miller
J. S. Fletcher
J. S. Knowles
J. Storer Clouston
J. W. Duffield
Jack London
Jacob Abbott
James Allen
James Andrews
James Baldwin

James Branch Cabell
James DeMille
James Joyce
James Lane Allen
James Lane Allen
James Oliver Curwood
James Oppenheim
James Otis
James R. Driscoll
Jane Abbott
Jane Austen
Jane L. Stewart
Janet Aldridge
Jens Peter Jacobsen
Jerome K. Jerome
Jessie Graham Flower
John Buchan
John Burroughs
John Cournos
John F. Kennedy
John Gay
John Glasworthy
John Habberton
John Joy Bell
John Kendrick Bangs
John Milton
John Philip Sousa
John Taintor Foote
Jonas Lauritz Idemil Lie
Jonathan Swift
Joseph A. Altsheler
Joseph Carey
Joseph Conrad
Joseph E. Badger Jr
Joseph Hergesheimer
Joseph Jacobs
Jules Vernes
Julian Hawthrone
Julie A Lippmann
Justin Huntly McCarthy
Kakuzo Okakura
Karle Wilson Baker
Kate Chopin
Kenneth Grahame
Kenneth McGaffey
Kate Langley Bosher
Kate Langley Bosher
Katherine Cecil Thurston
Katherine Stokes
L. A. Abbot
L. T. Meade

L. Frank Baum	Owen Johnson	Stephen Crane
Latta Griswold	P.G. Wodehouse	Stewart Edward White
Laura Dent Crane	Paul and Mabel Thorne	Stijn Streuvels
Laura Lee Hope	Paul G. Tomlinson	Swami Abhedananda
Laurence Housman	Paul Severing	Swami Parmananda
Lawrence Beasley	Percy Brebner	T. S. Ackland
Leo Tolstoy	Percy Keese Fitzhugh	T. S. Arthur
Leonid Andreyev	Peter B. Kyne	The Princess Der Ling
Lewis Carroll	Plato	Thomas A. Janvier
Lewis Sperry Chafer	Quincy Allen	Thomas A Kempis
Lilian Bell	R. Derby Holmes	Thomas Anderton
Lloyd Osbourne	R. L. Stevenson	Thomas Bailey Aldrich
Louis Hughes	R. S. Ball	Thomas Bulfinch
Louis Joseph Vance	Rabindranath Tagore	Thomas De Quincey
Louis Tracy	Rahul Alvares	Thomas Dixon
Louisa May Alcott	Ralph Bonehill	Thomas H. Huxley
Lucy Fitch Perkins	Ralph Henry Barbour	Thomas Hardy
Lucy Maud Montgomery	Ralph Victor	Thomas More
Luther Benson	Ralph Waldo Emmerson	Thornton W. Burgess
Lydia Miller Middleton	Rene Descartes	U. S. Grant
Lyndon Orr	Ray Cummings	Upton Sinclair
M. Corvus	Rex Beach	Valentine Williams
M. H. Adams	Rex E. Beach	Various Authors
Margaret E. Sangster	Richard Harding Davis	Vaughan Kester
Margret Howth	Richard Jefferies	Victor Appleton
Margaret Vandercook	Richard Le Gallienne	Victor G. Durham
Margaret W. Hungerford	Robert Barr	Victoria Cross
Margret Penrose	Robert Frost	Virginia Woolf
Maria Edgeworth	Robert Gordon Anderson	Wadsworth Camp
Maria Thompson Daviess	Robert L. Drake	Walter Camp
Mariano Azuela	Robert Lansing	Walter Scott
Marion Polk Angellotti	Robert Lynd	Washington Irving
Mark Overton	Robert Michael Ballantyne	Wilbur Lawton
Mark Twain	Robert W. Chambers	Wilkie Collins
Mary Austin	Rosa Nouchette Carey	Willa Cather
Mary Catherine Crowley	Rudyard Kipling	Willard F. Baker
Mary Cole	Saint Augustine	William Dean Howells
Mary Hastings Bradley	Samuel B. Allison	William le Queux
Mary Roberts Rinehart	Samuel Hopkins Adams	W. Makepeace Thackeray
Mary Rowlandson	Sarah Bernhardt	William W. Walter
M. Wollstonecraft Shelley	Sarah C. Hallowell	William Shakespeare
Maud Lindsay	Selma Lagerlof	Winston Churchill
Max Beerbohm	Sherwood Anderson	Yei Theodora Ozaki
Myra Kelly	Sigmund Freud	Yogi Ramacharaka
Nathaniel Hawthrone	Standish O'Grady	Young E. Allison
Nicolo Machiavelli	Stanley Weyman	Zane Grey
O. F. Walton	Stella Benson	
Oscar Wilde	Stella M. Francis